This Coloring book Belongs to:

_____

Sugar Skulls - CopyRights 2020 Papa Abdou Books, Authour, Illustrator, or Publishing info.

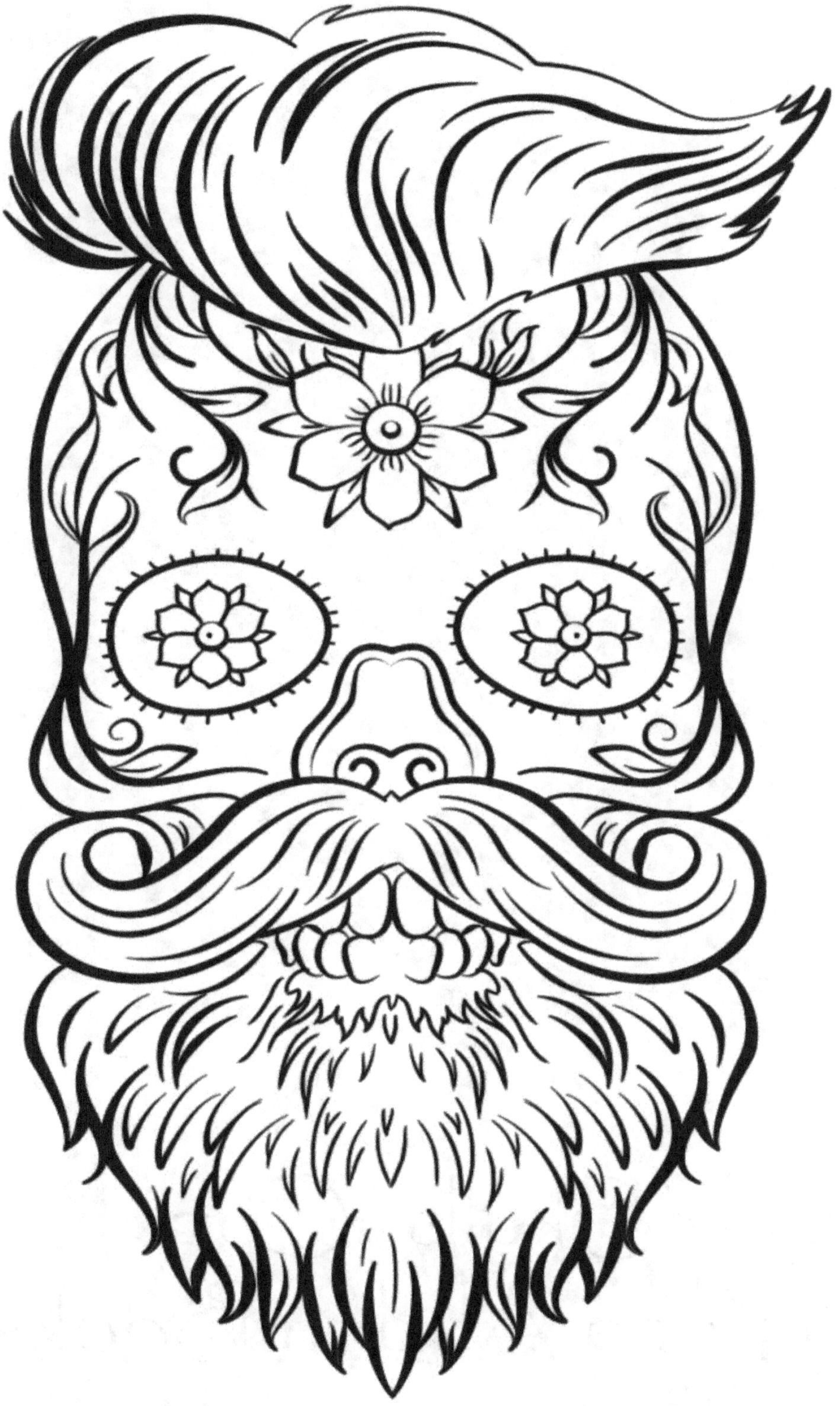

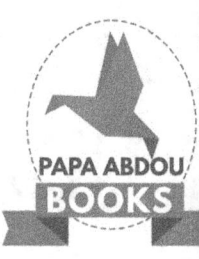

Sugar Skulls - CopyRights 2020 Papa Abdou Books, Authour, Illustrator, or Publishing info.

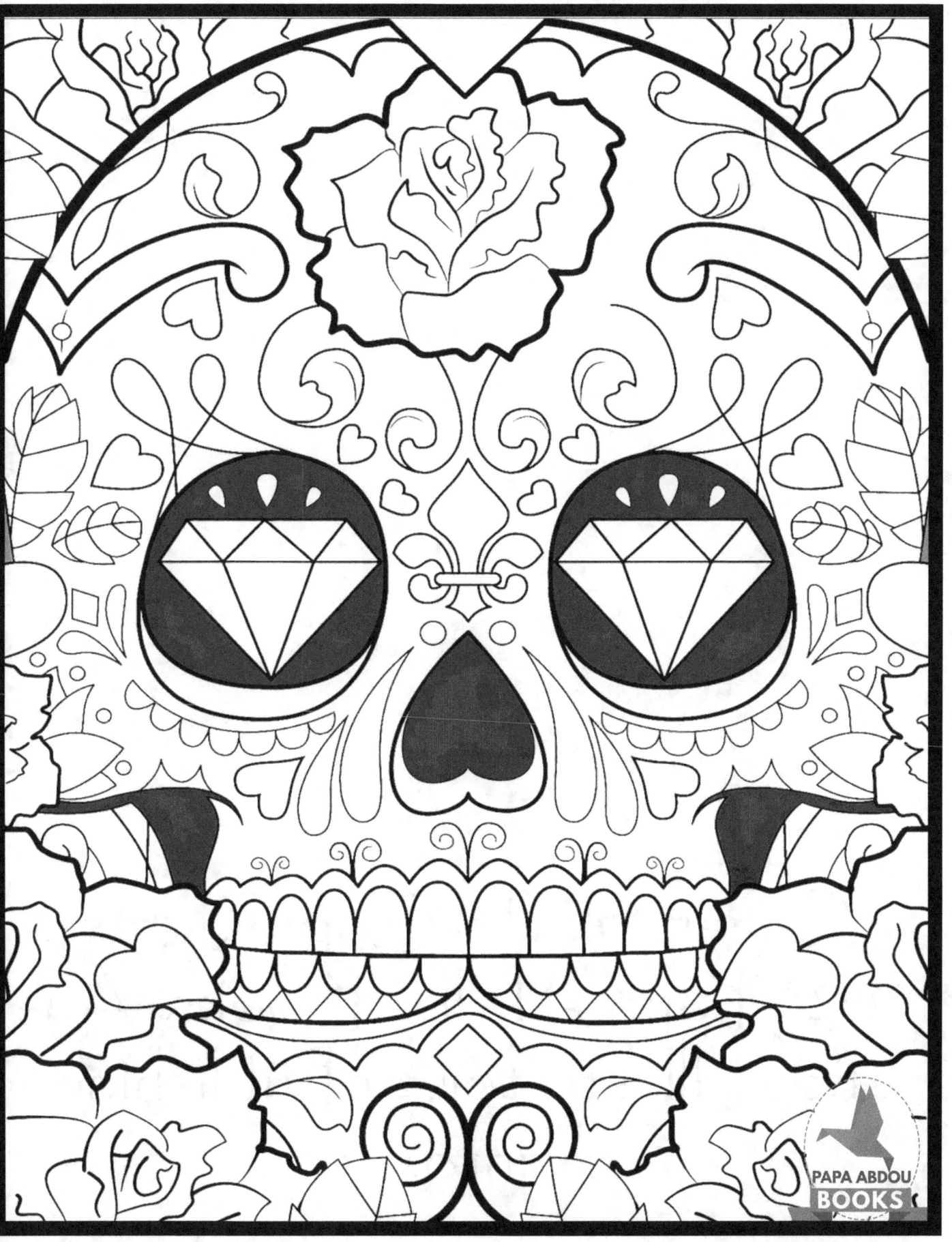

Sugar Skulls - CopyRights 2020 Papa Abdou Books, Authour, Illustrator, or Publishing info.

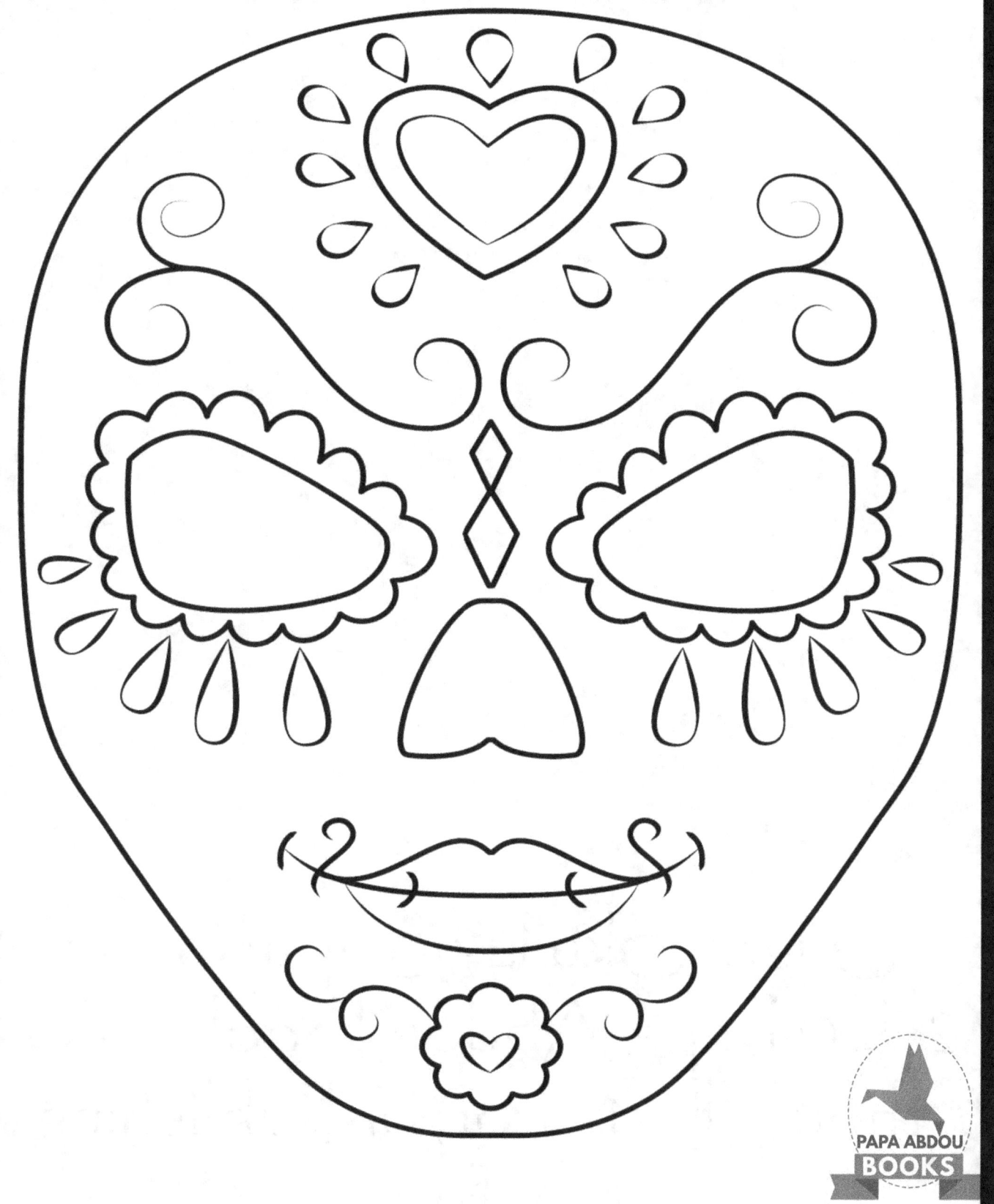

Sugar Skulls -CopyRights 2020 Papa Abdou Books, Authour, Illustrator, or Publishing info.

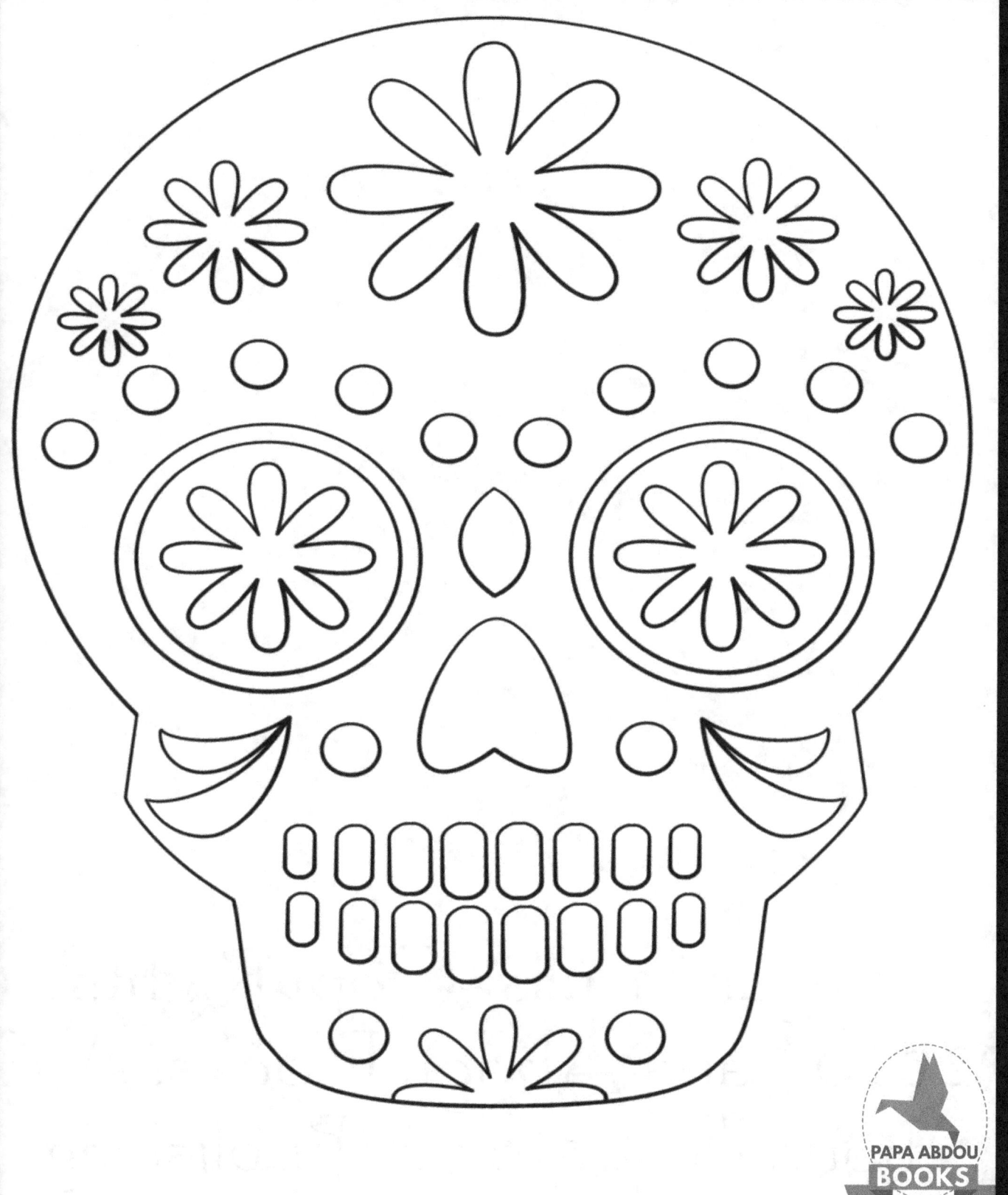

Sugar Skulls - CopyRights 2020 Papa Abdou Books, Authour, Illustrator, or Publishing info.

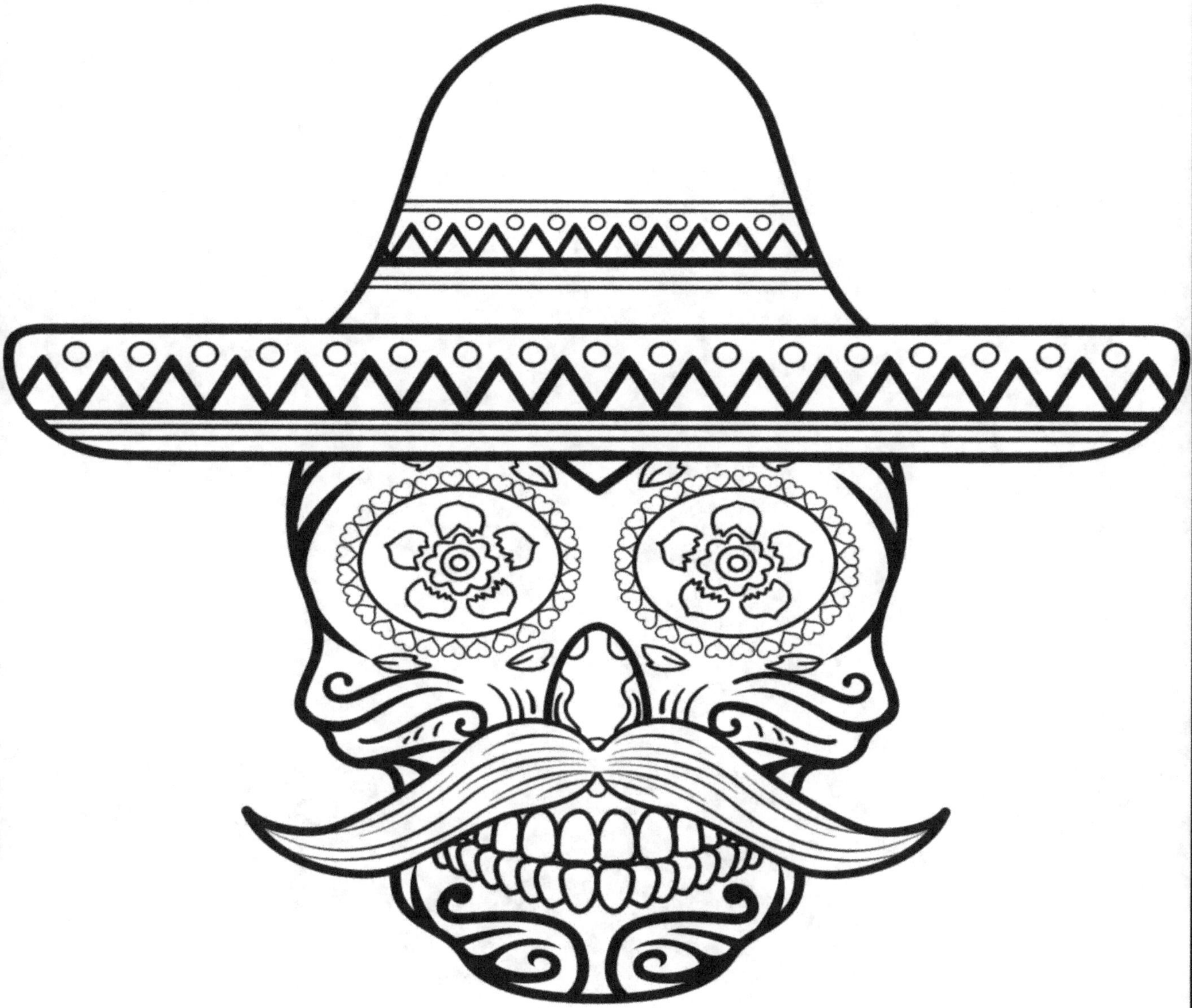

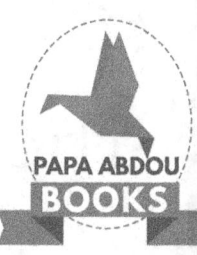

Sugar Skulls - CopyRights 2020 Papa Abdou Books, Authour, Illustrator, or Publishing info.

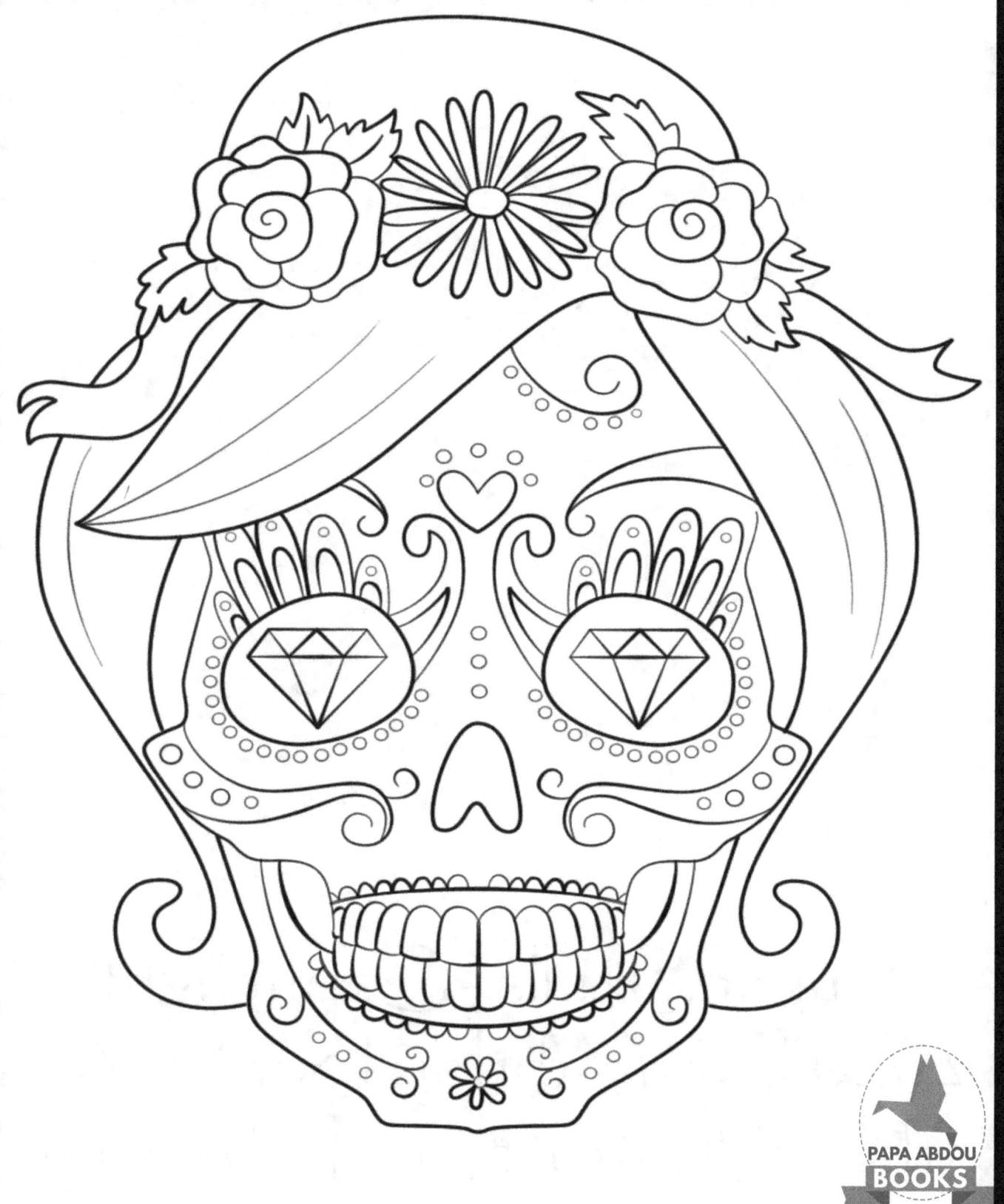

Sugar Skulls - CopyRights 2020 Papa Abdou Books, Authour, Illustrator, or Publishing info.

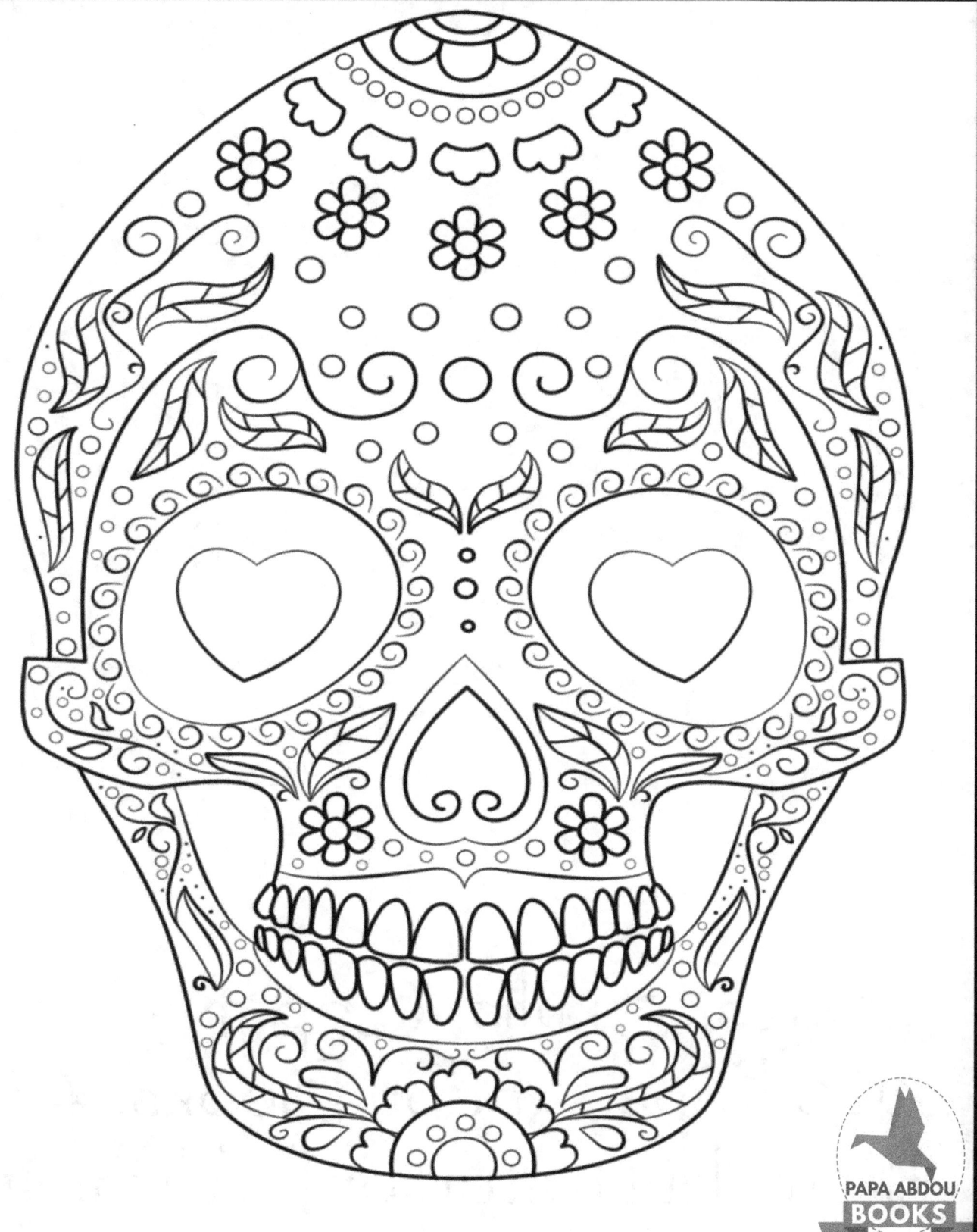

Sugar Skulls - CopyRights 2020 Papa Abdou Books, Authour, Illustrator, or Publishing info.

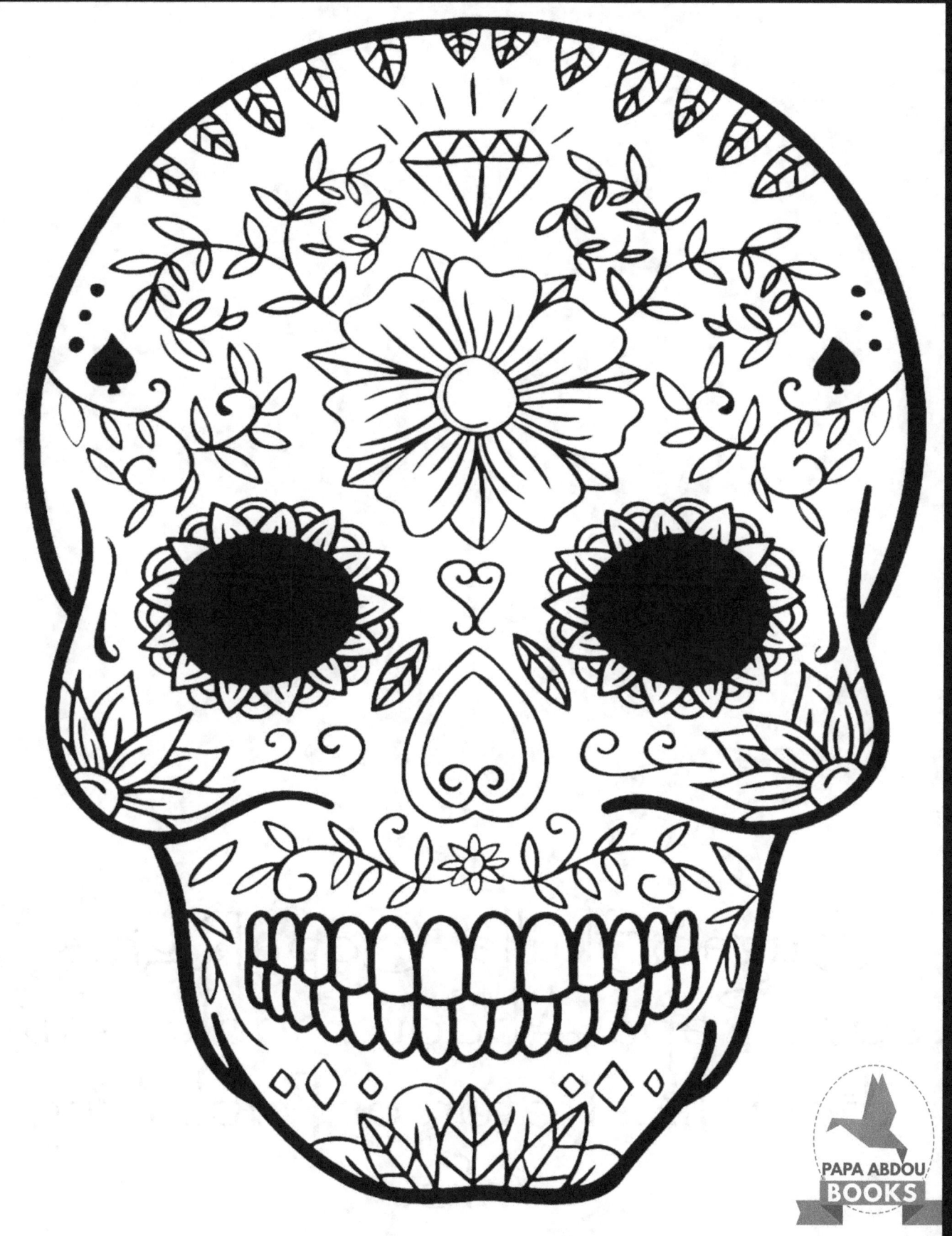

Sugar Skulls - CopyRights 2020 Papa Abdou Books, Authour, Illustrator, or Publishing info.

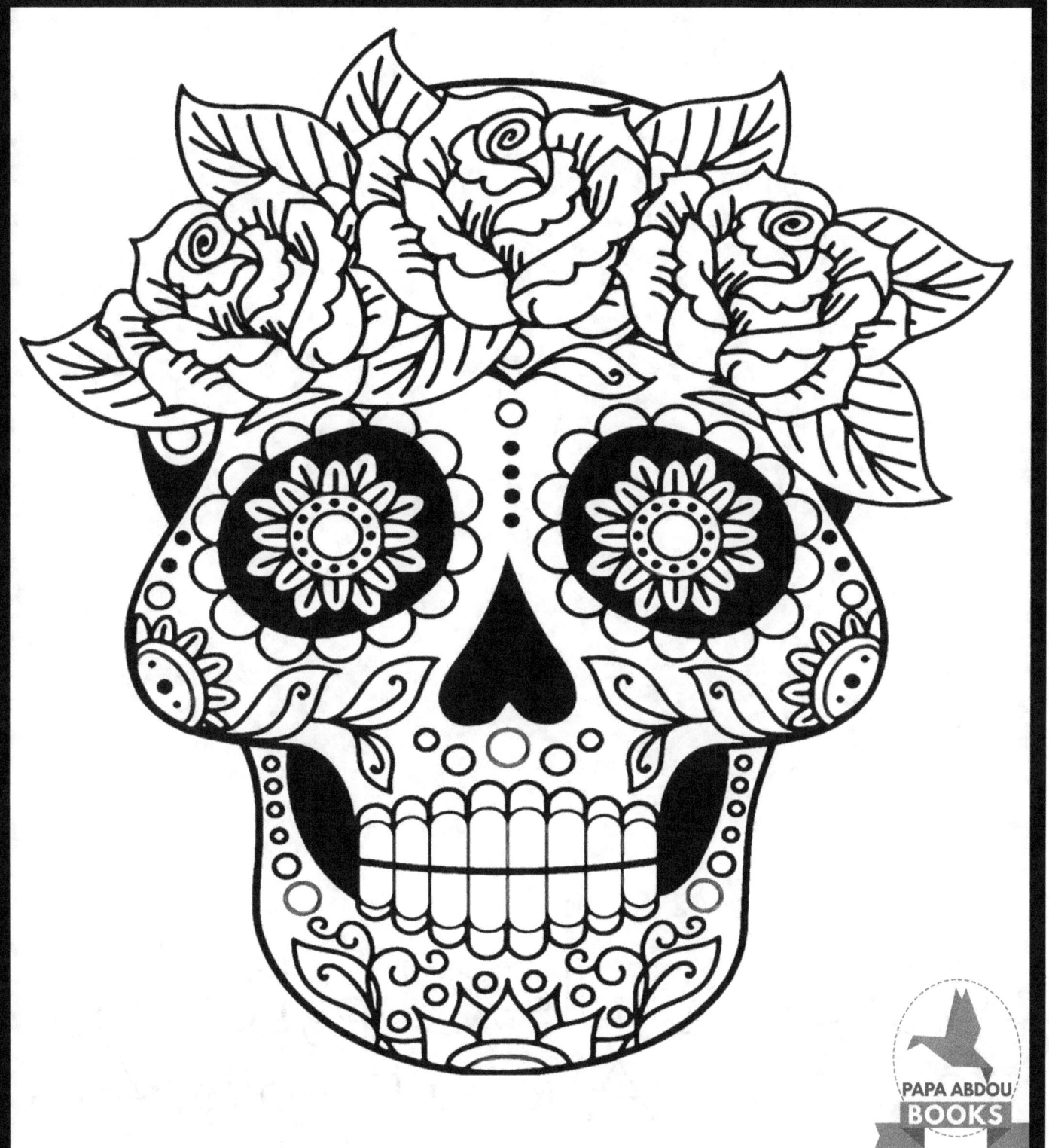

Sugar Skulls -CopyRights 2020 Papa Abdou Books, Authour, Illustrator, or Publishing info.

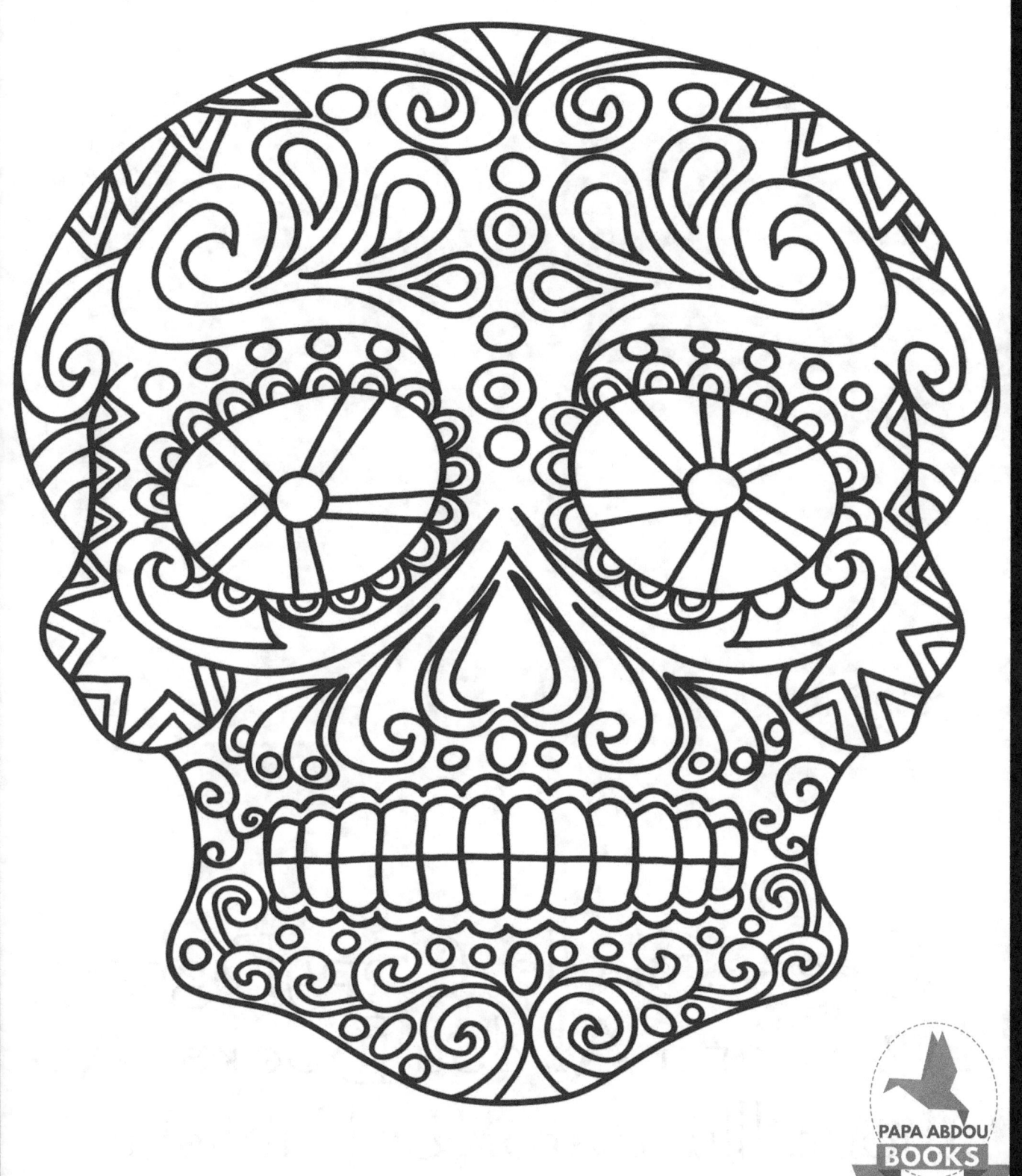

Sugar Skulls - CopyRights 2020 Papa Abdou Books, Authour, Illustrator, or Publishing info.

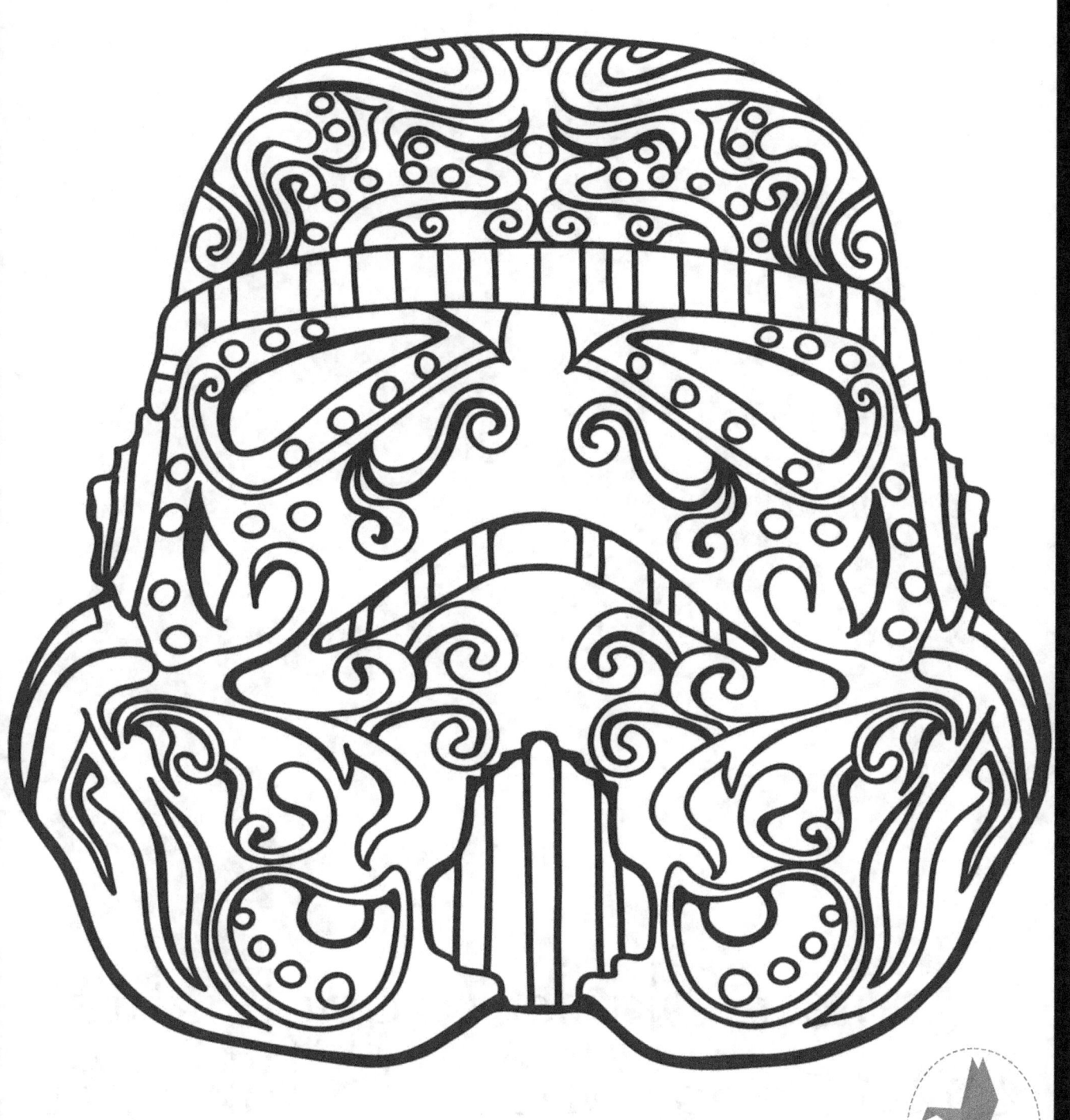

Sugar Skulls - CopyRights 2020 Papa Abdou Books, Authour, Illustrator, or Publishing info.

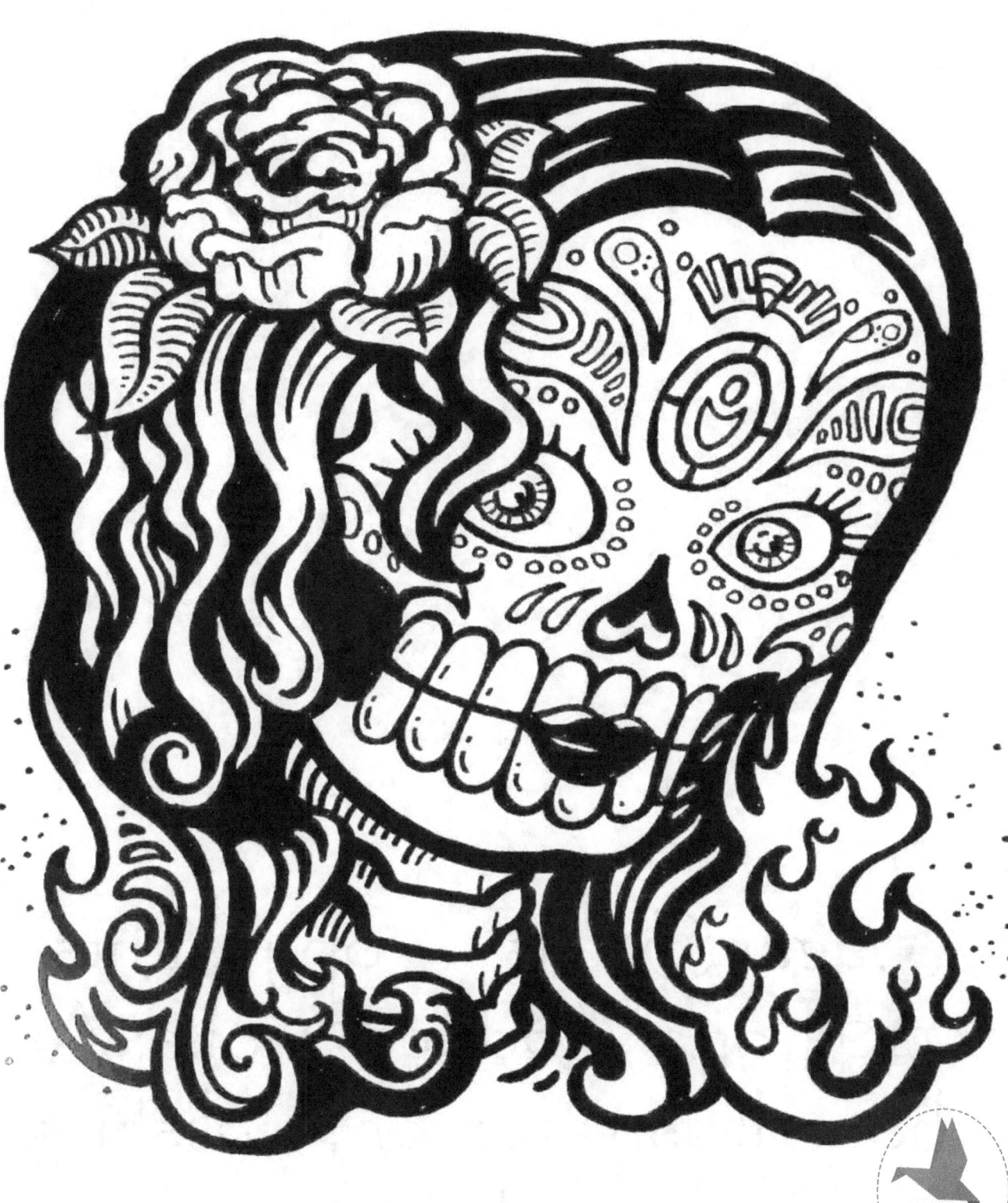

Sugar Skulls -CopyRights 2020 Papa Abdou Books, Authour, Illustrator, or Publishing info.

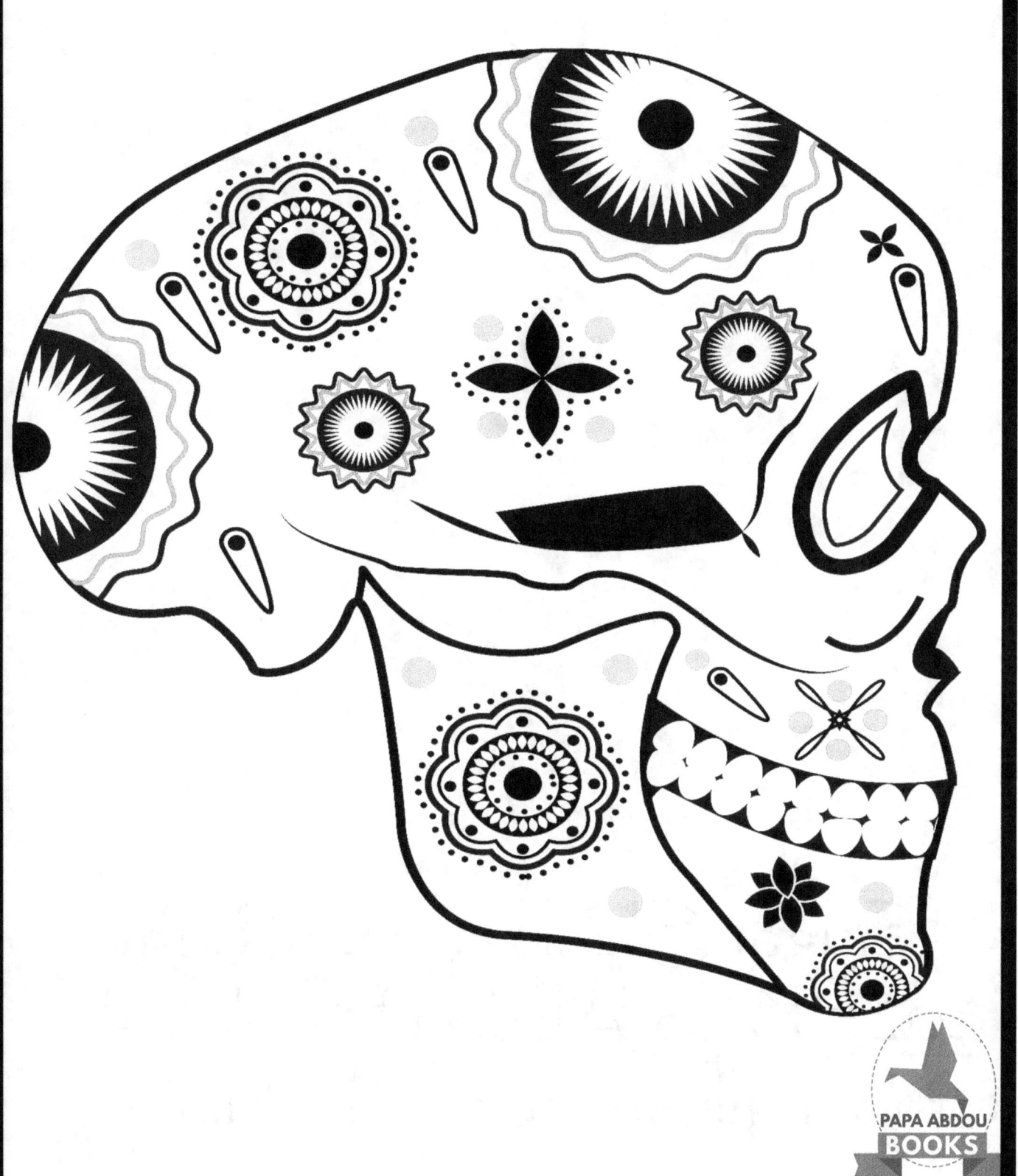

Sugar Skulls -CopyRights 2020 Papa Abdou Books, Authour, Illustrator, or Publishing info.

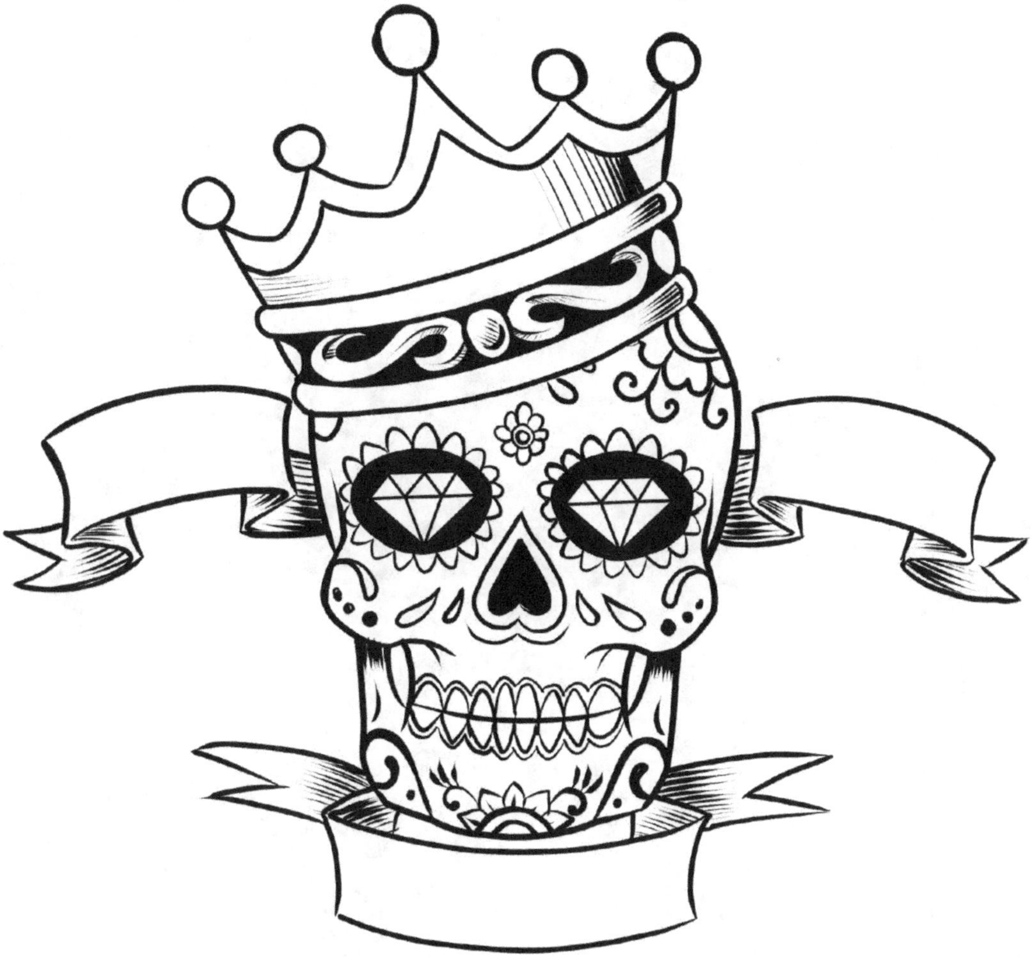

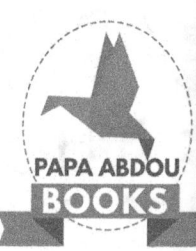

Sugar Skulls - CopyRights 2020 Papa Abdou Books, Authour, Illustrator, or Publishing info.

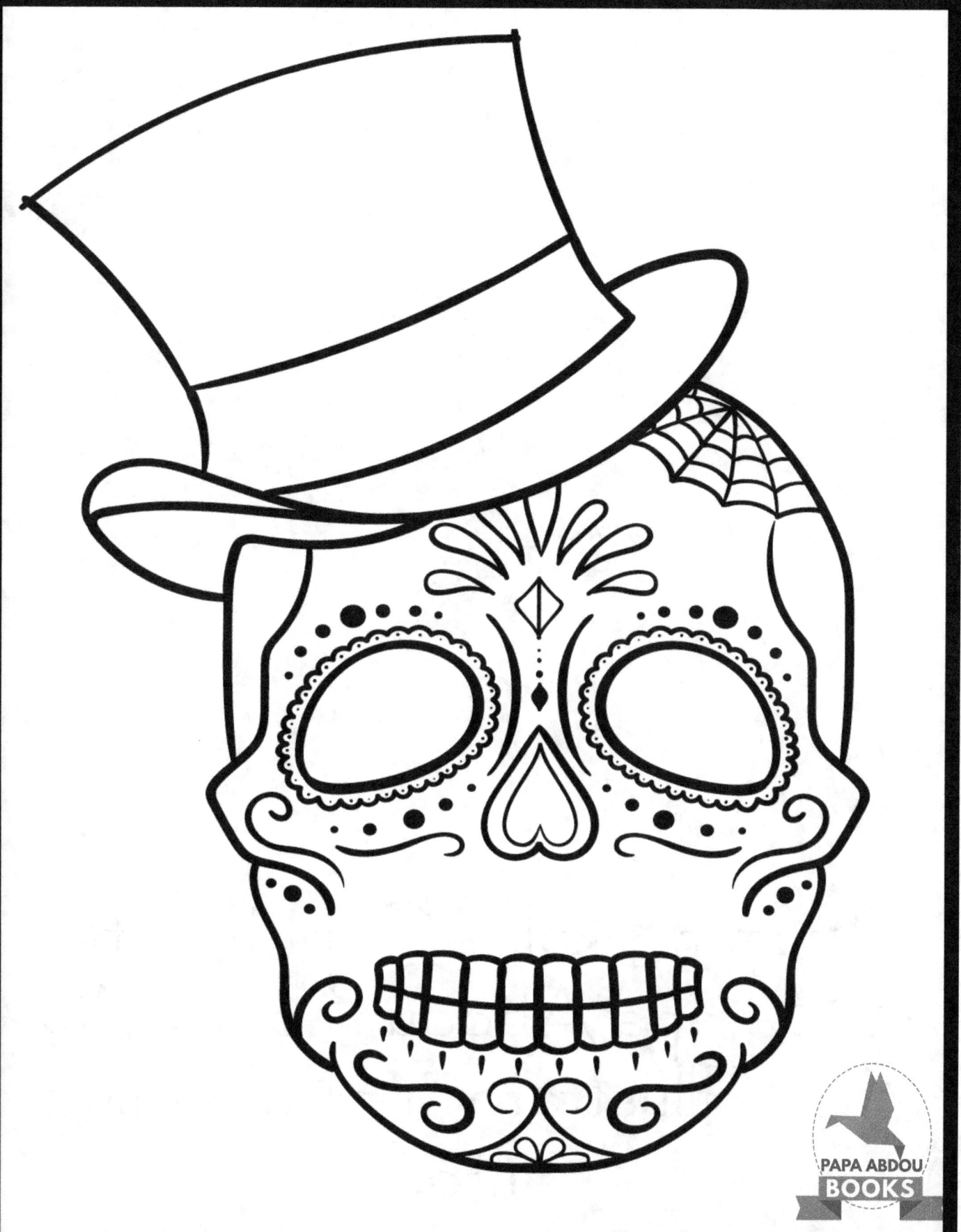

Sugar Skulls -CopyRights 2020 Papa Abdou Books, Authour, Illustrator, or Publishing info.

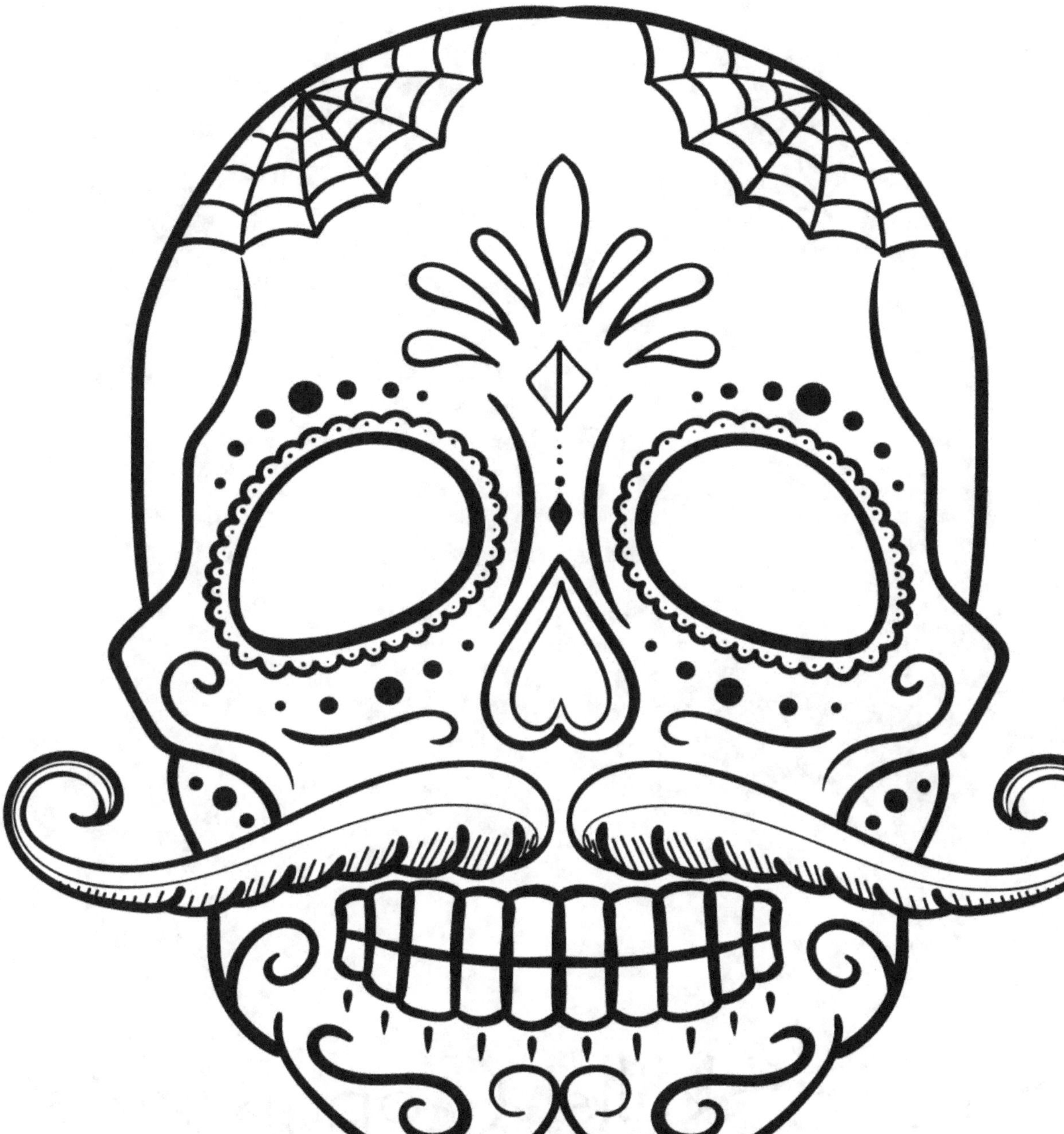

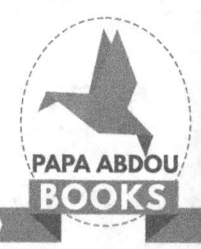

Sugar Skulls - CopyRights 2020 Papa Abdou Books, Authour, Illustrator, or Publishing info.

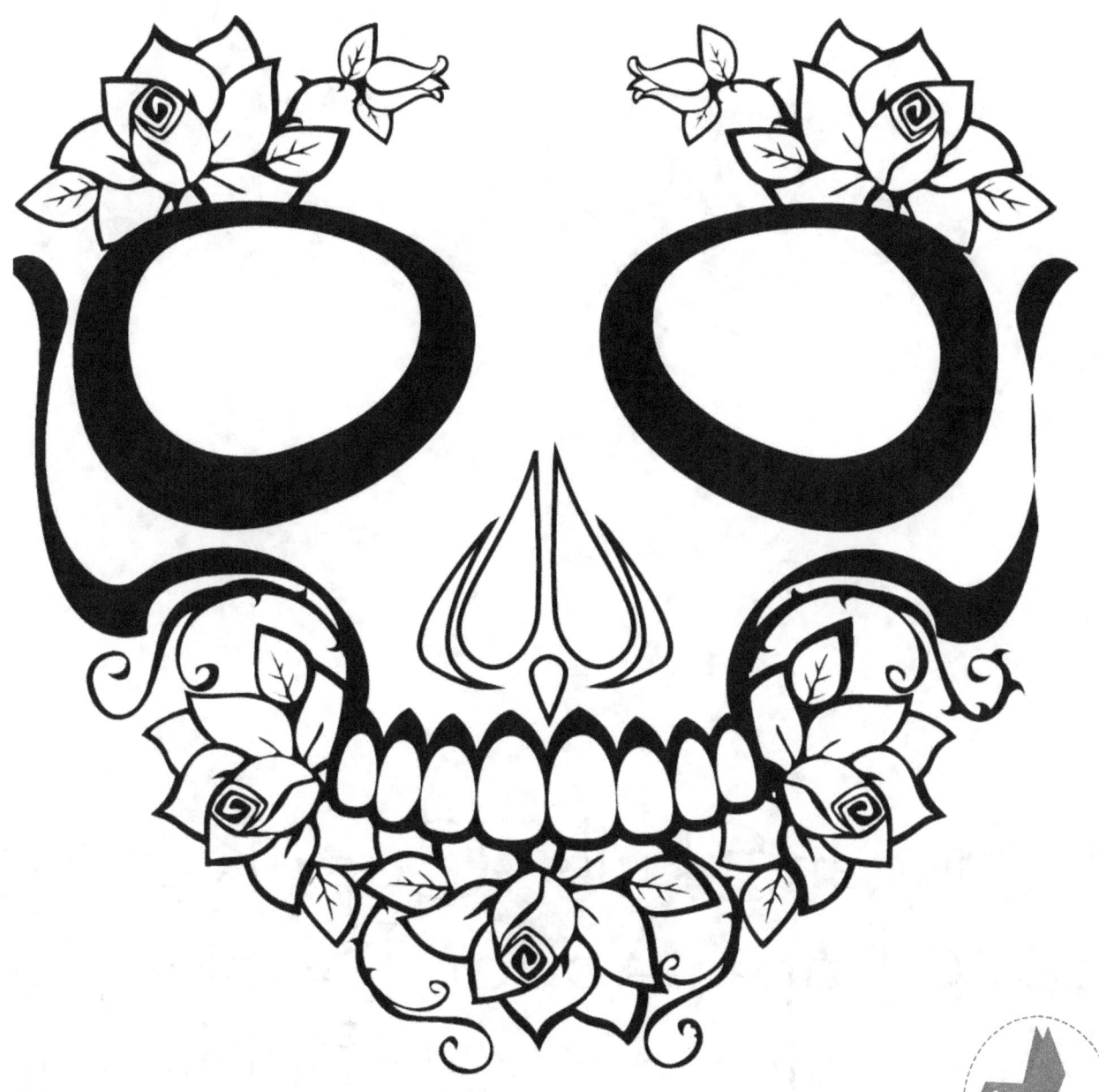

Sugar Skulls - CopyRights 2020 Papa Abdou Books, Authour, Illustrator, or Publishing info.

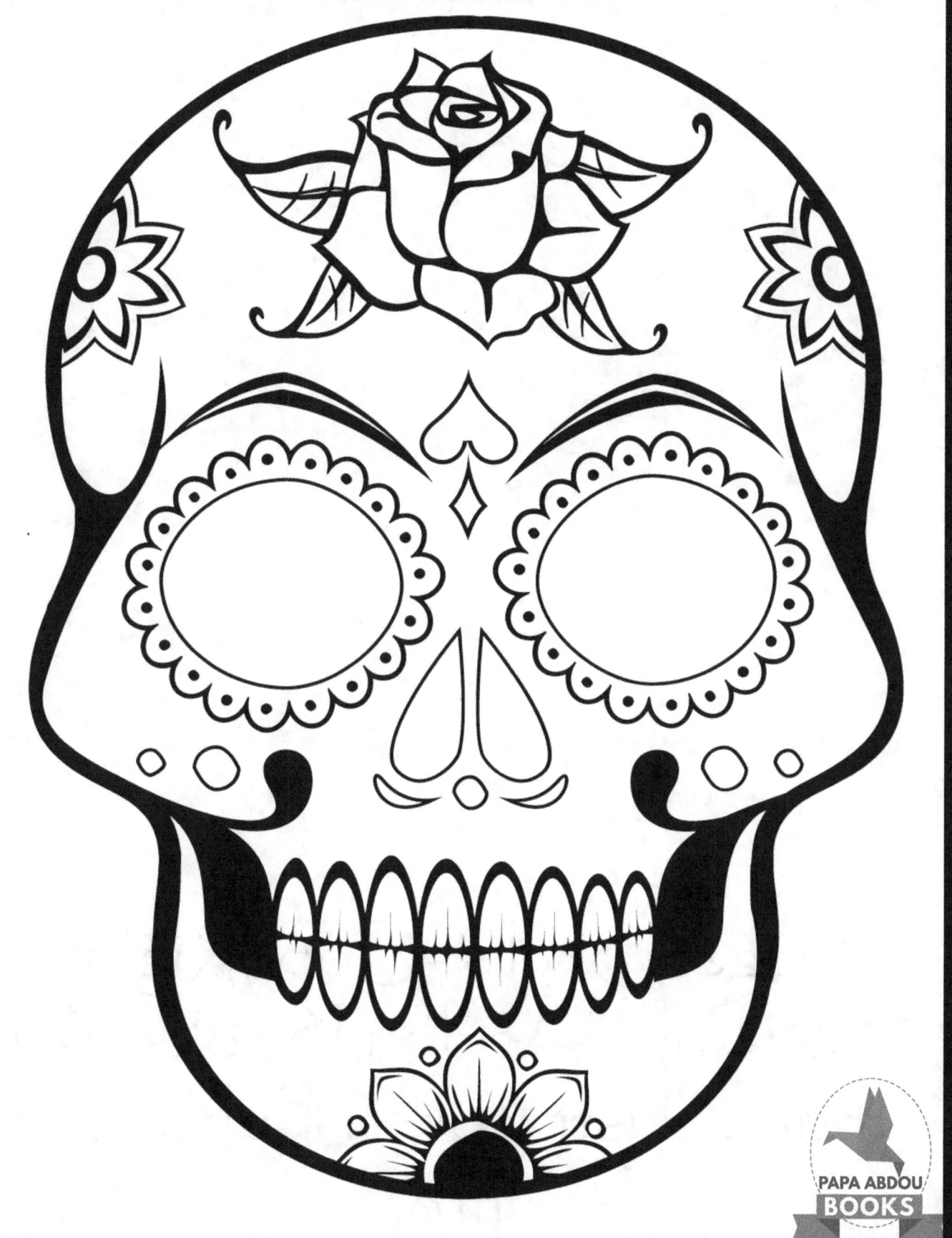

Sugar Skulls -CopyRights 2020 Papa Abdou Books, Authour, Illustrator, or Publishing info.

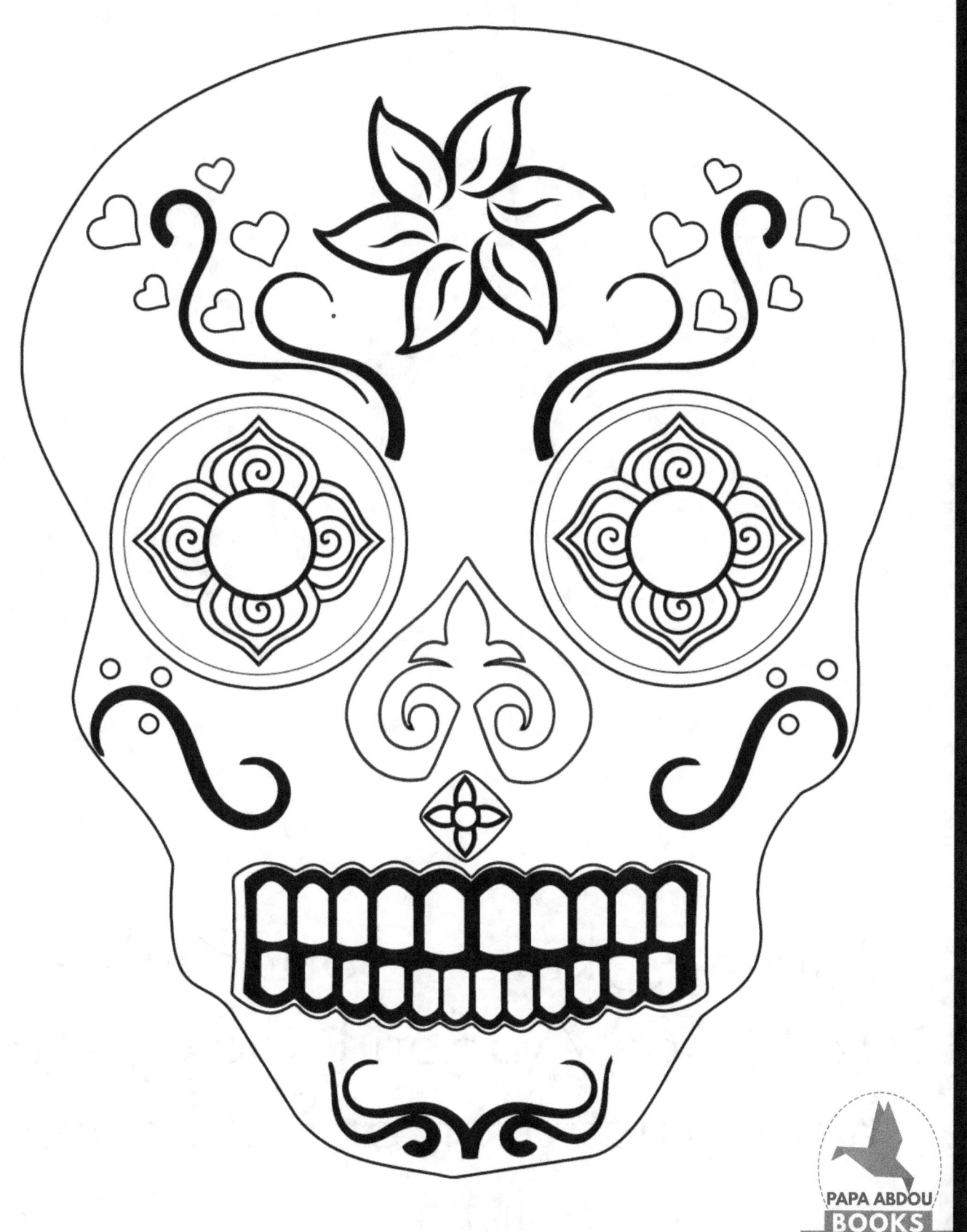

Sugar Skulls - CopyRights 2020 Papa Abdou Books, Authour, Illustrator, or Publishing info.

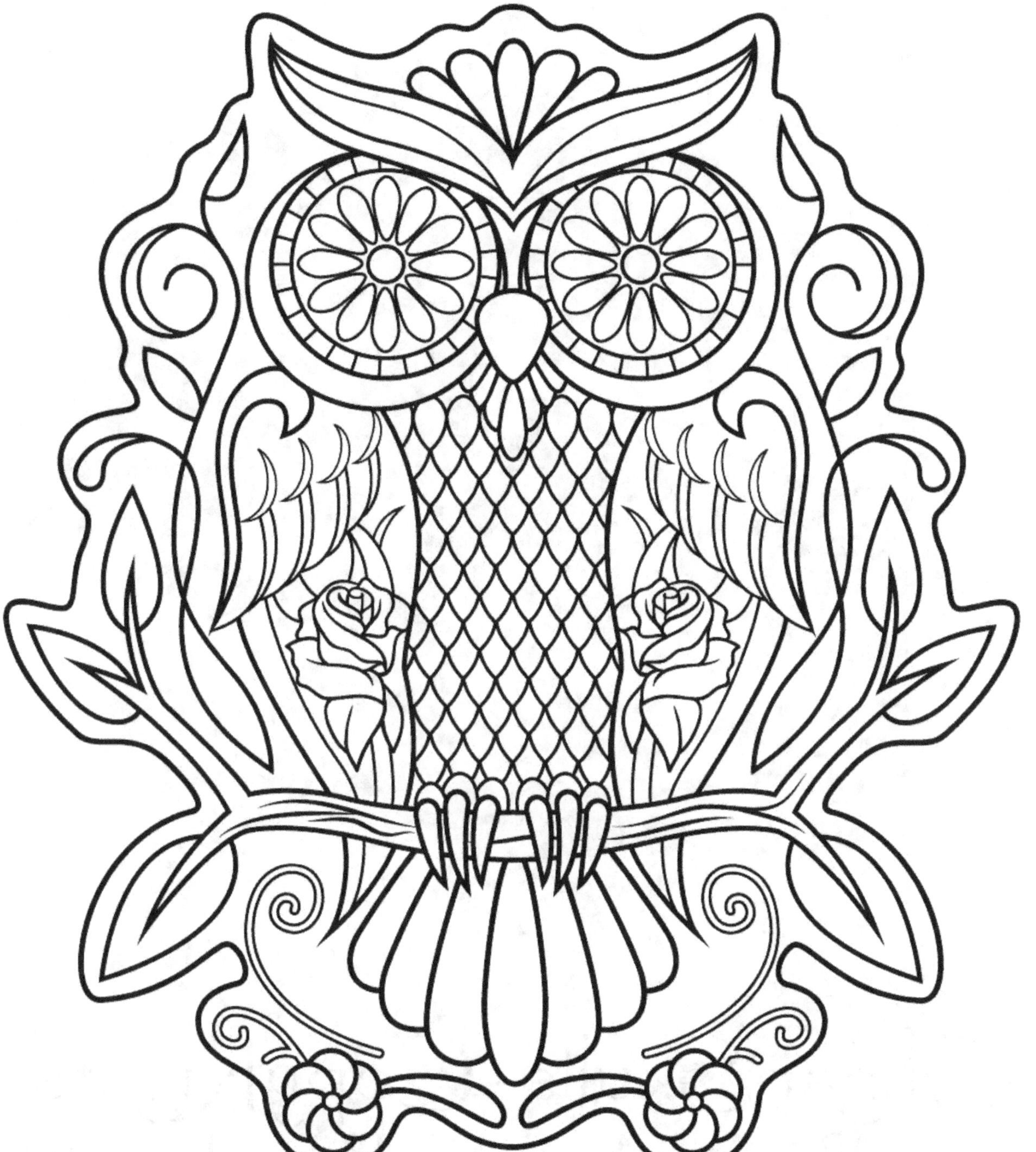

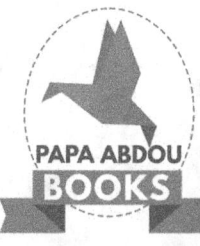

Sugar Skulls -CopyRights 2020 Papa Abdou Books, Authour, Illustrator, or Publishing info.

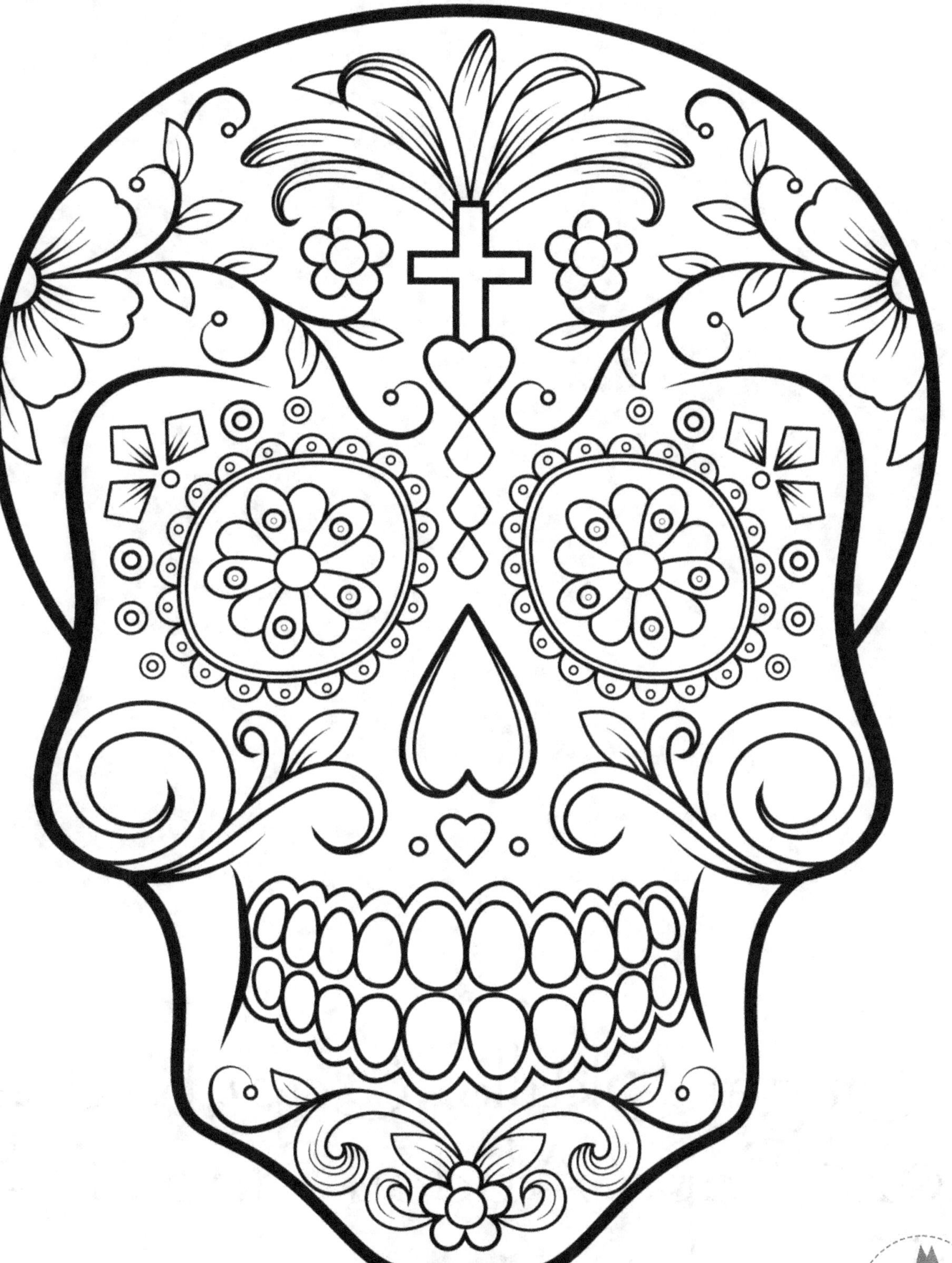

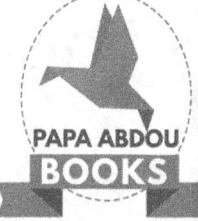

Sugar Skulls - CopyRights 2020 Papa Abdou Books, Authour, Illustrator, or Publishing info.

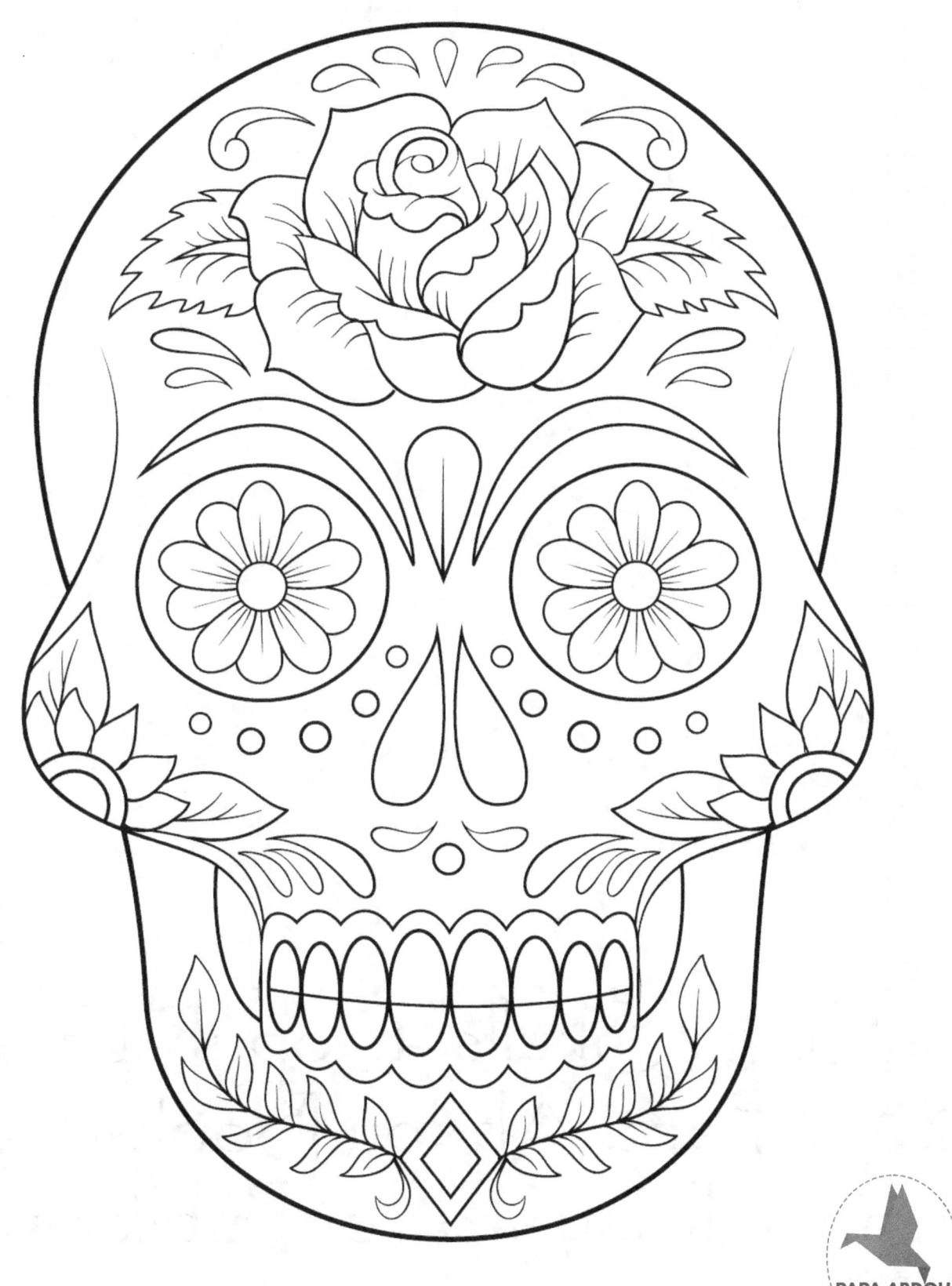

Sugar Skulls - CopyRights 2020 Papa Abdou Books, Authour, Illustrator, or Publishing info.

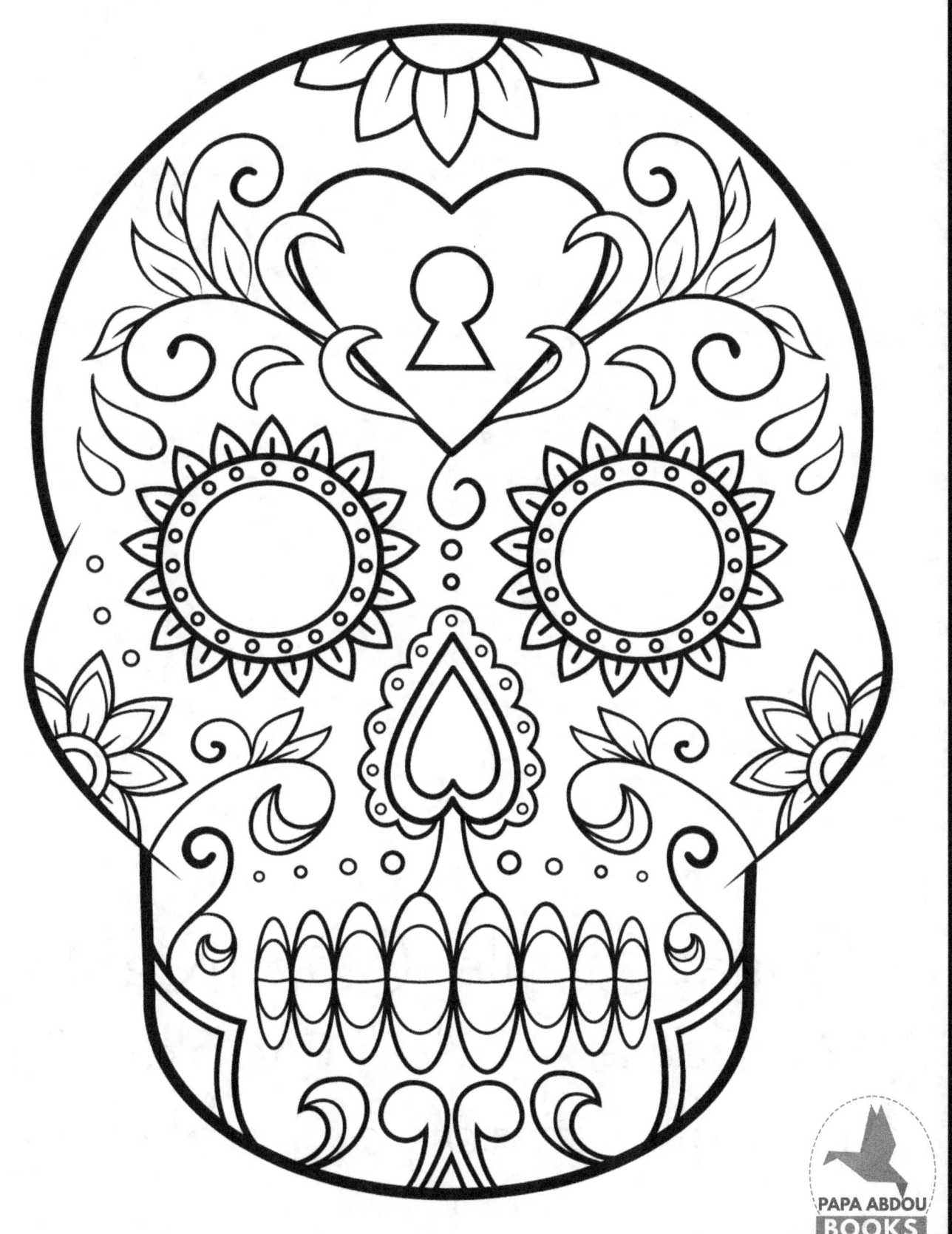

Sugar Skulls -CopyRights 2020 Papa Abdou Books, Authour, Illustrator, or Publishing info.

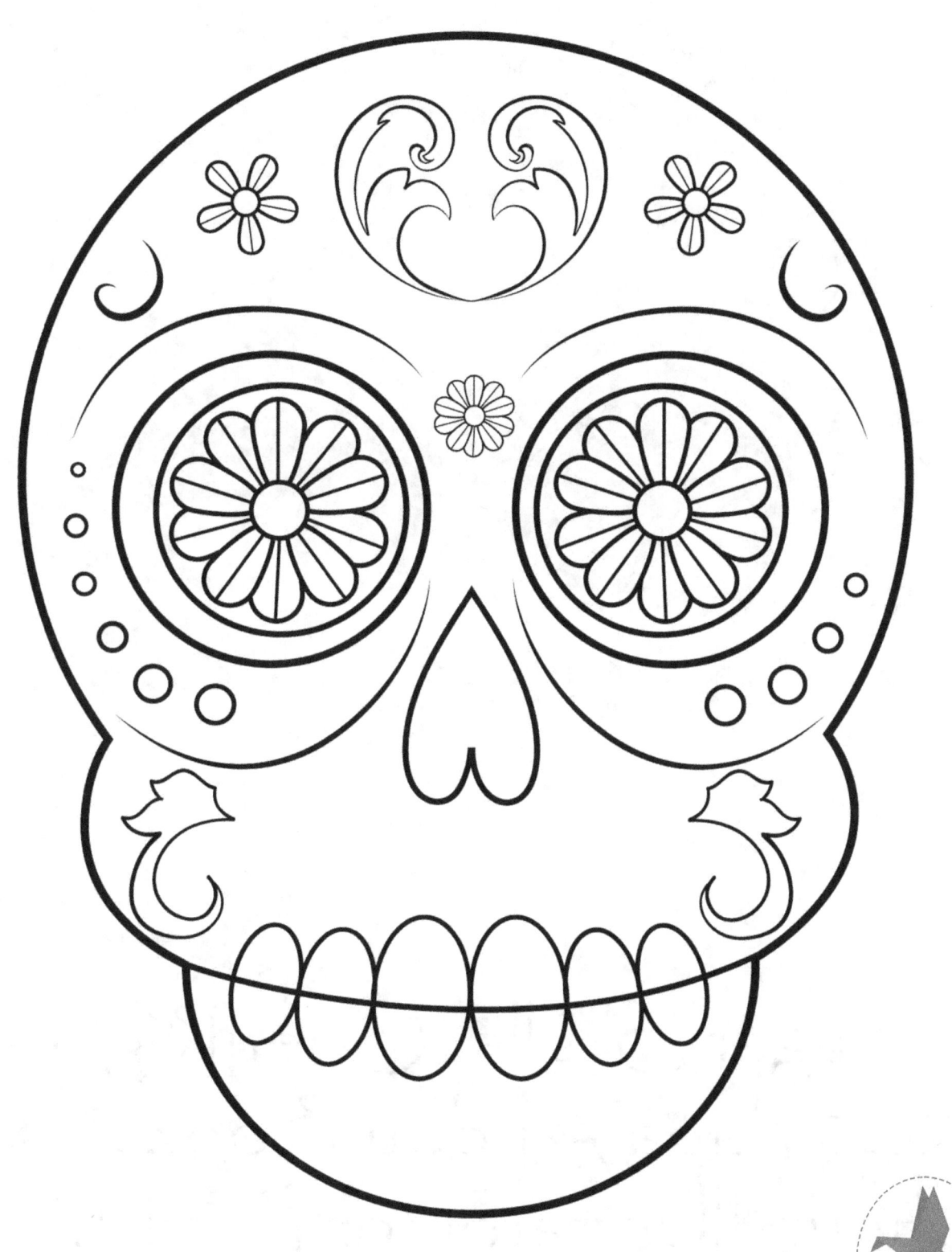

Sugar Skulls -CopyRights 2020 Papa Abdou Books, Authour, Illustrator, or Publishing info.

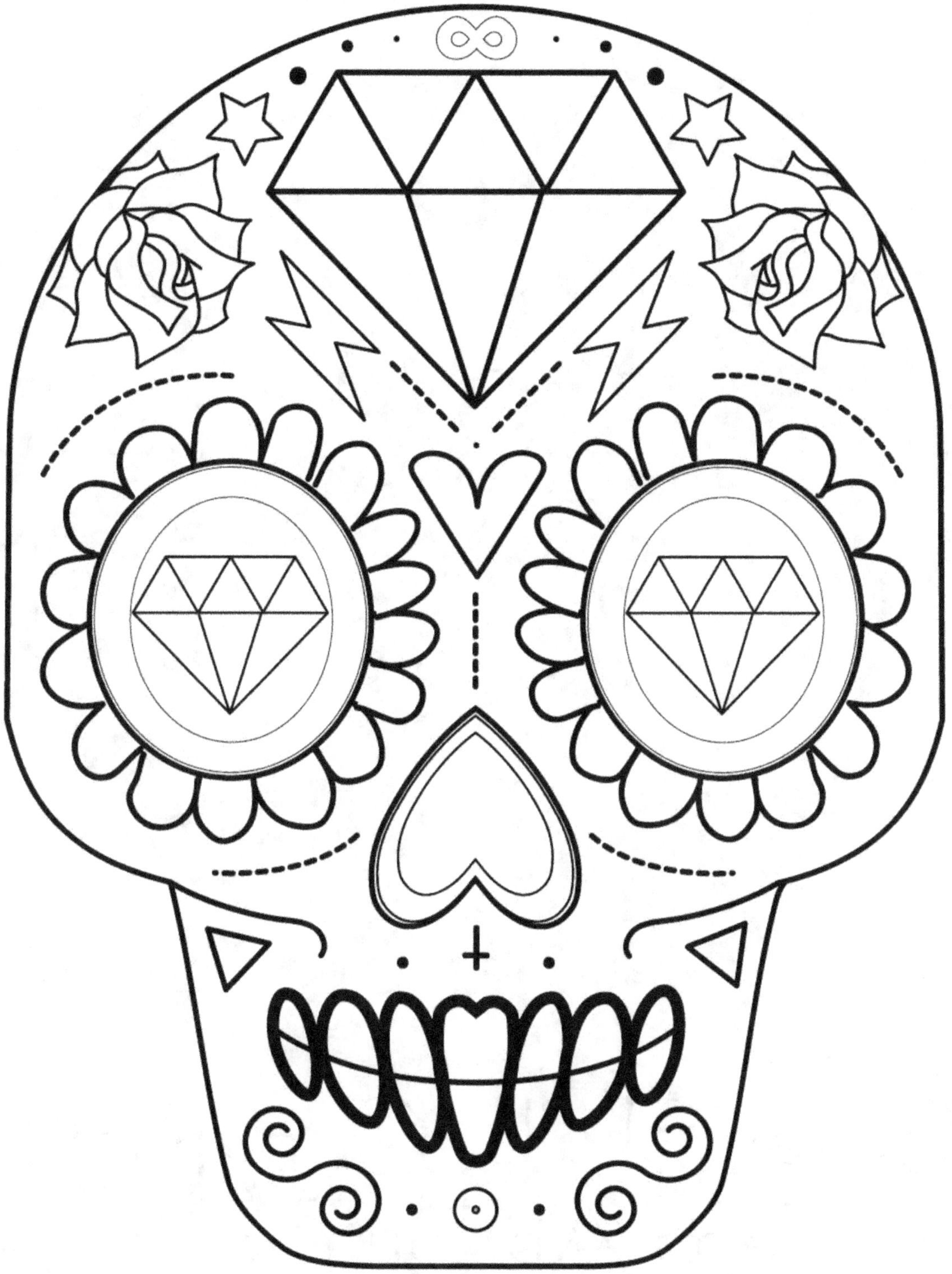

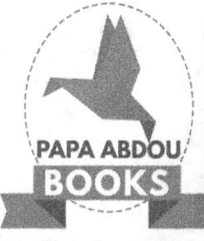

Sugar Skulls - CopyRights 2020 Papa Abdou Books, Authour, Illustrator, or Publishing info.

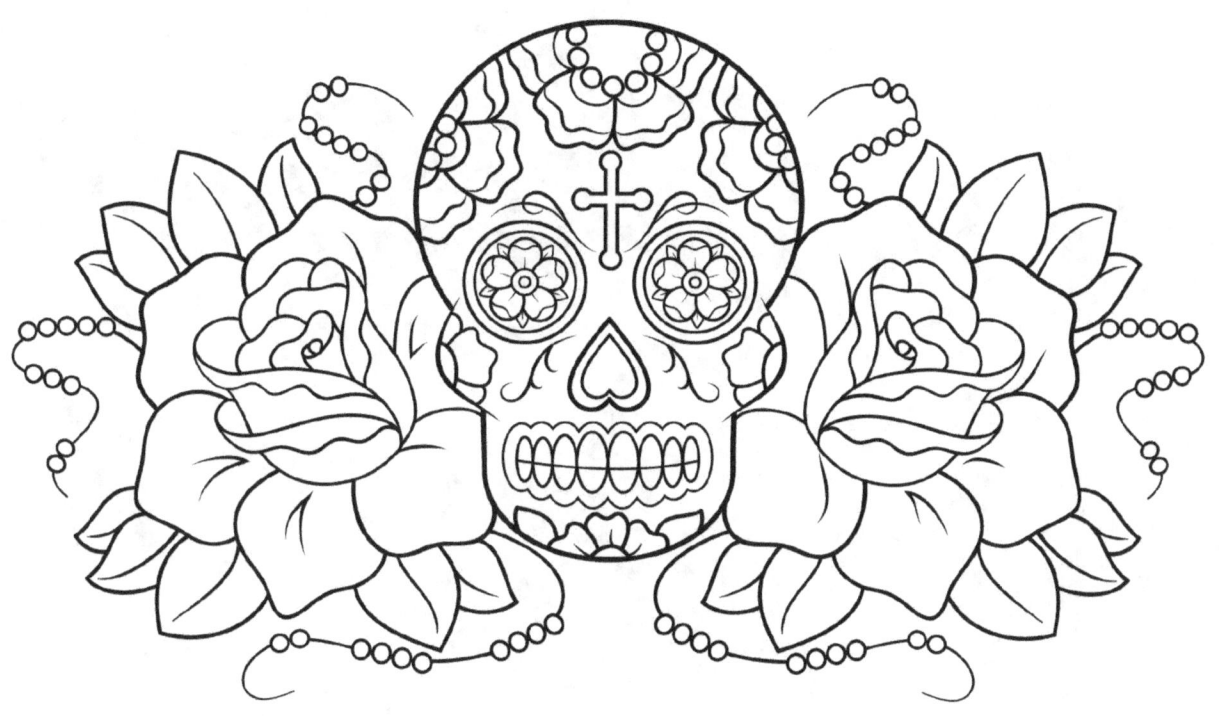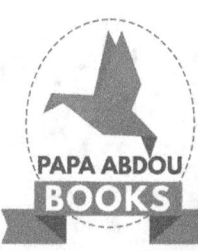

Sugar Skulls - CopyRights 2020 Papa Abdou Books, Authour, Illustrator, or Publishing info.

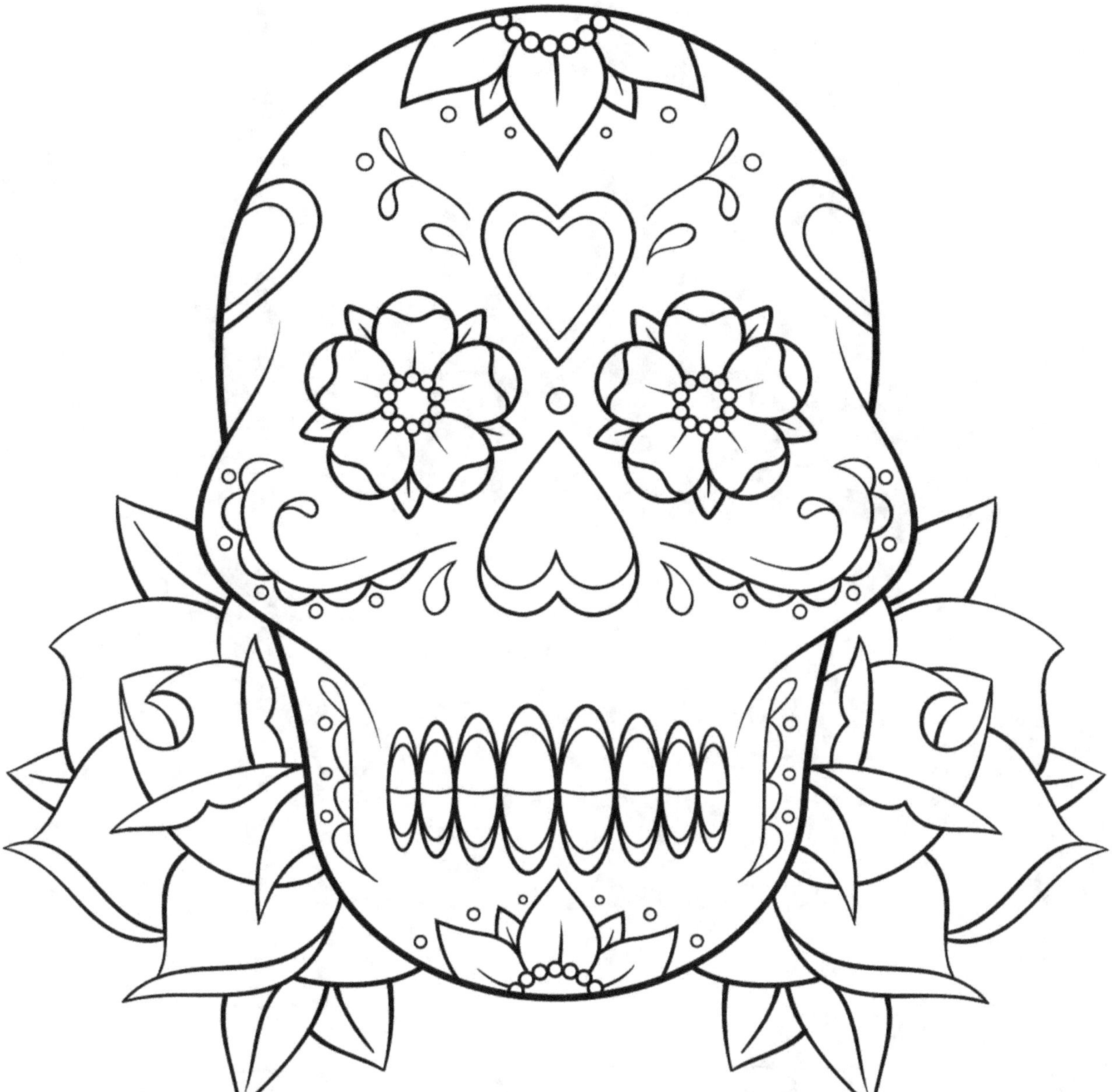

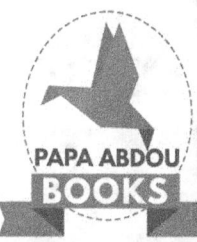

Sugar Skulls - CopyRights 2020 Papa Abdou Books, Authour, Illustrator, or Publishing info.

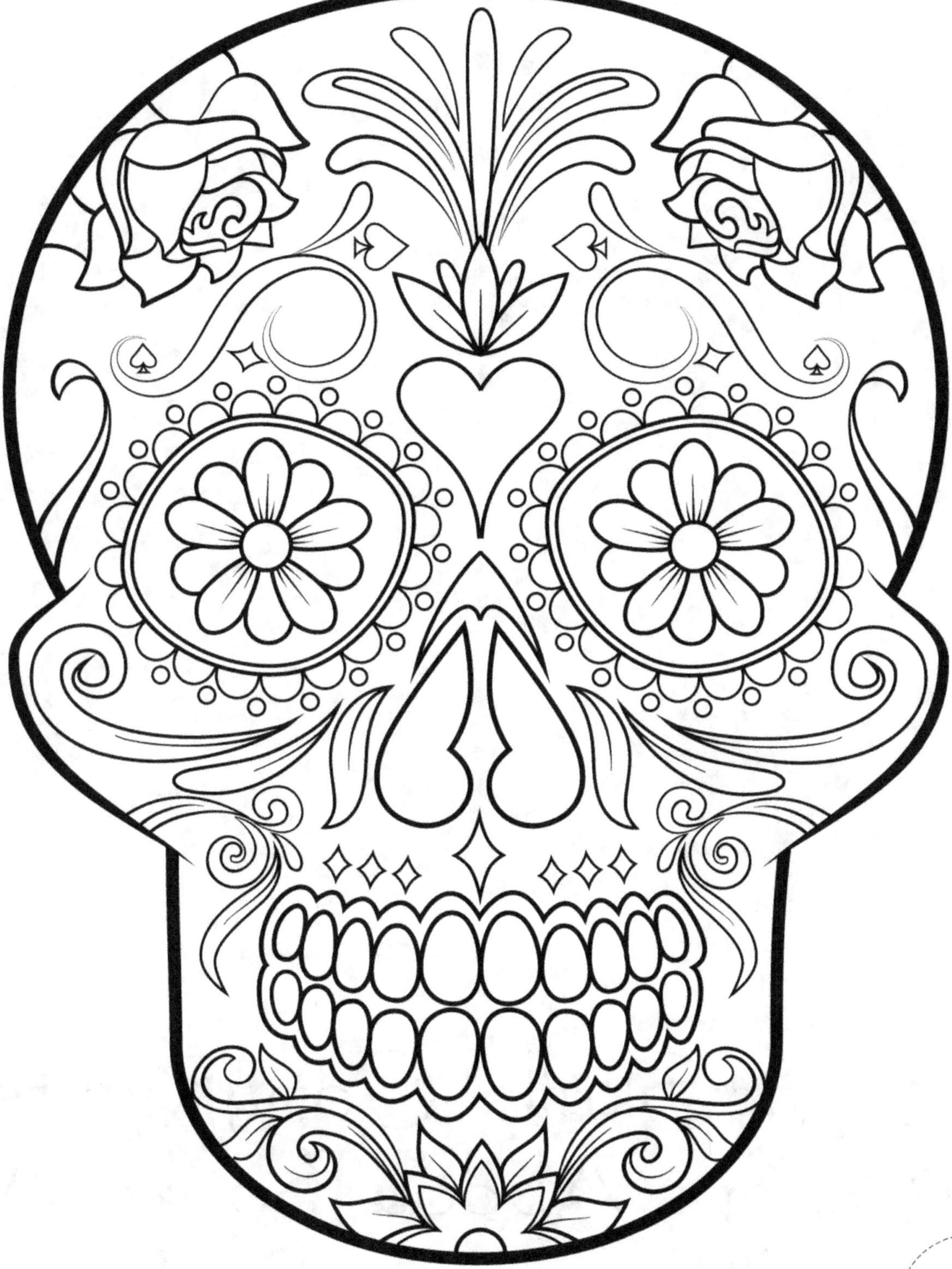

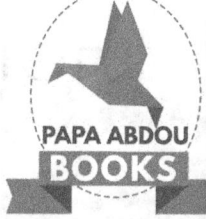

Sugar Skulls -CopyRights 2020 Papa Abdou Books, Authour, Illustrator, or Publishing info.

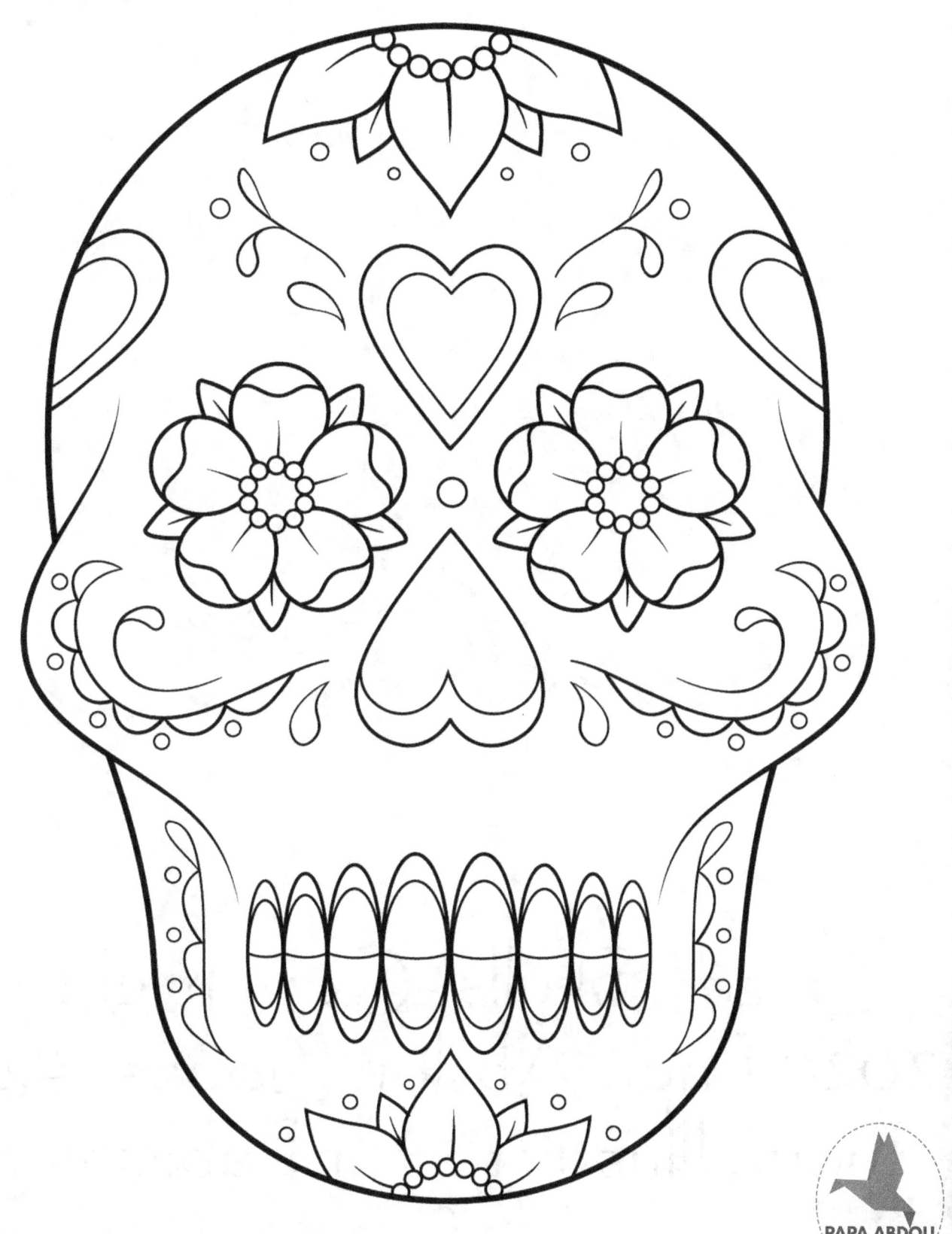

Sugar Skulls - CopyRights 2020 Papa Abdou Books, Authour, Illustrator, or Publishing info.

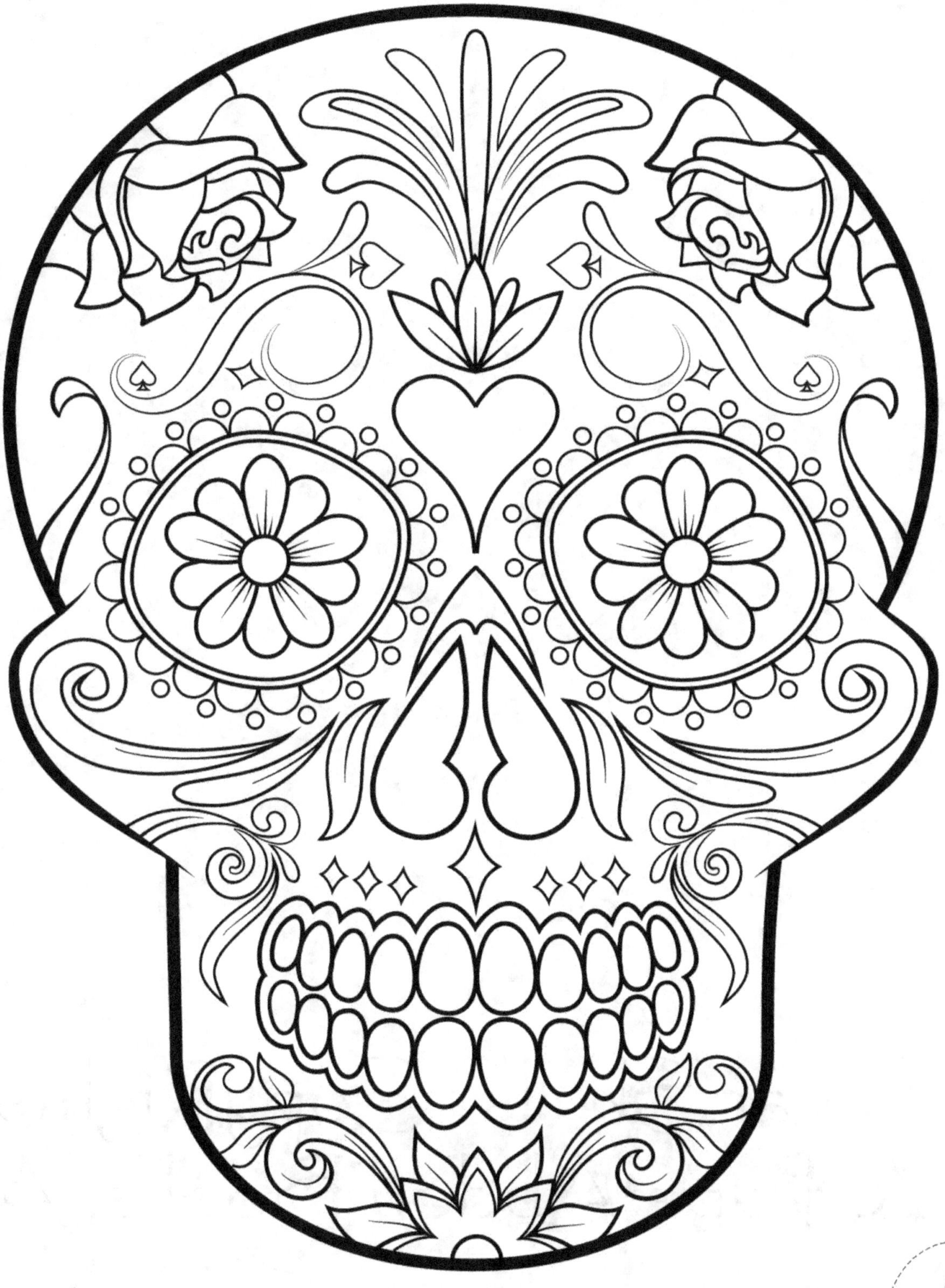

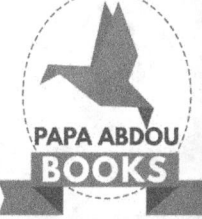

Sugar Skulls - CopyRights 2020 Papa Abdou Books, Authour, Illustrator, or Publishing info.

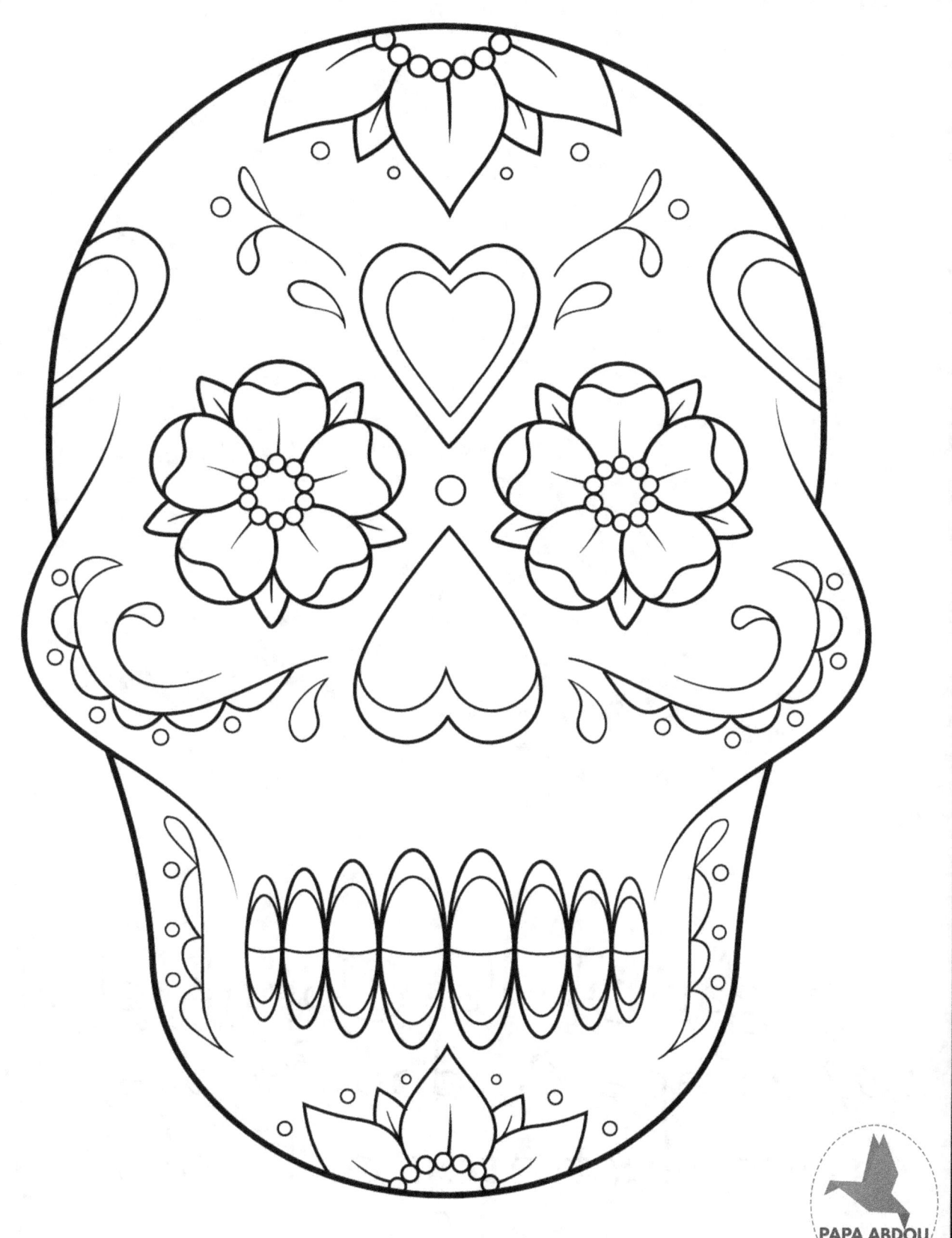

Sugar Skulls -CopyRights 2020 Papa Abdou Books, Authour, Illustrator, or Publishing info.

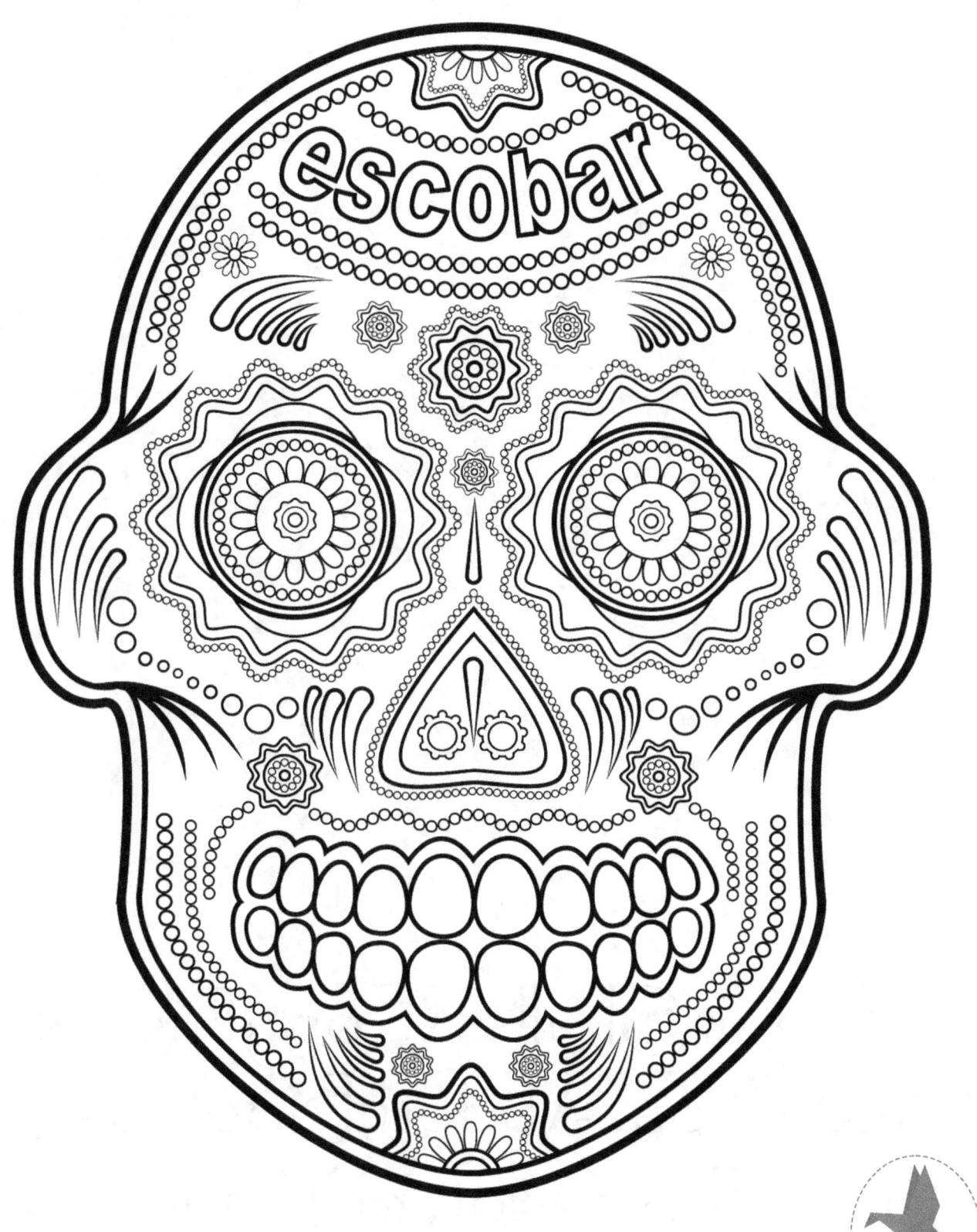

Sugar Skulls -CopyRights 2020 Papa Abdou Books, Authour, Illustrator, or Publishing info.

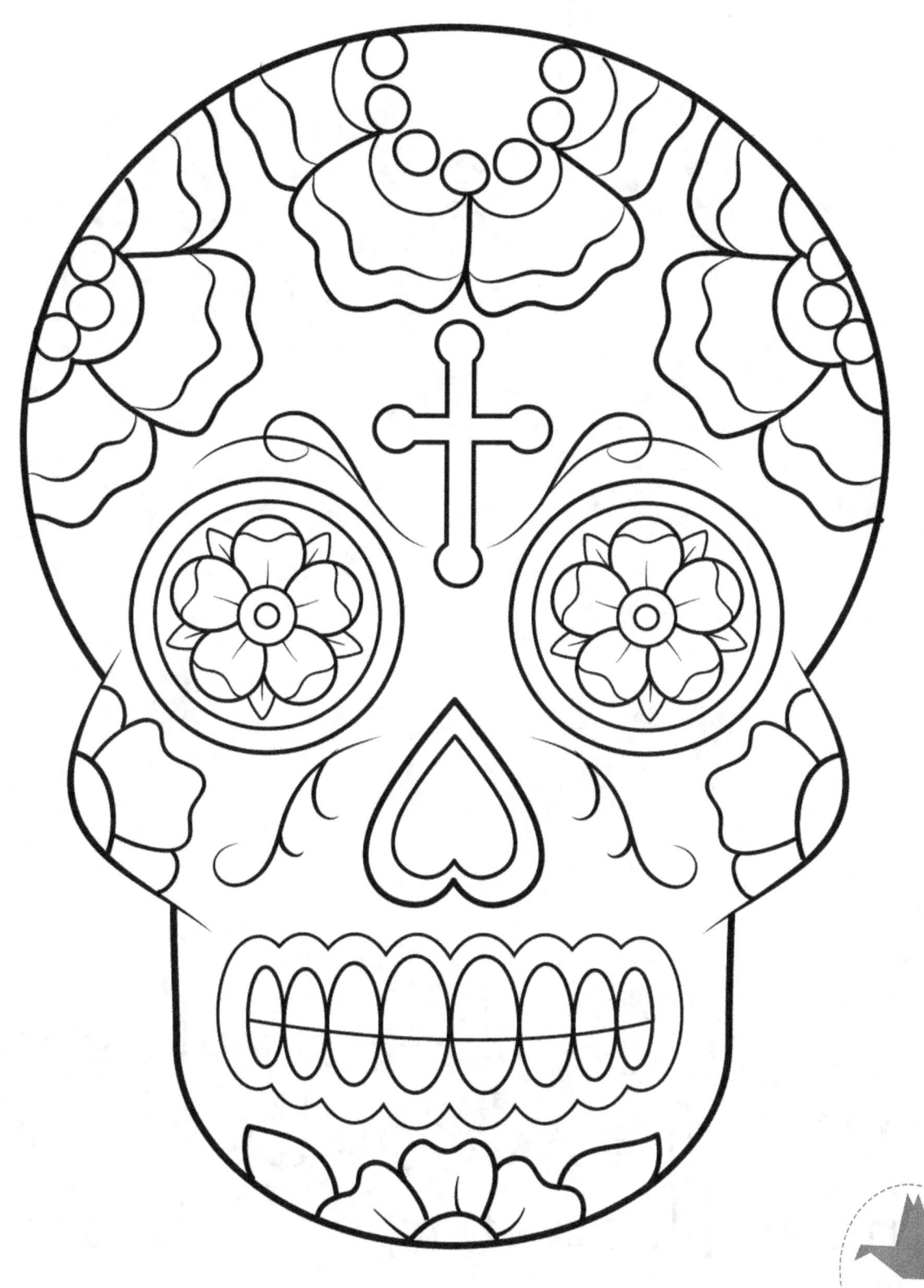

Sugar Skulls - CopyRights 2020 Papa Abdou Books, Authour, Illustrator, or Publishing info.

www.ingramcontent.com/pod-product-compliance
Lightning Source LLC
Chambersburg PA
CBHW081458220526
45466CB00008B/2693